# The Strange

LHP

## Written or Edited by Thomas D. Perry

*Ascent To Glory: The Genealogy of J. E. B. Stuart*
*The Free State of Patrick: Patrick County Virginia In The Civil War*
*"The Dear Old Hills of Patrick:" J. E. B. Stuart and Patrick County VA*
*God's Will Be Done: The Christian Life of J. E. B. Stuart*
*"Whatever May Be My Fate, May You Be Happy"*
*The Papers of J. E. B. Stuart Volume One 1833-54*
*Images of America: Patrick County Virginia*
*Images of America: Henry County Virginia*
*Then and Now: Patrick County Virginia*
*Notes From The Free State Of Patrick*
*Patrick County Oral History Project: A Guide*
*Fire on Bull Mountain*
*Patrick County Virginia's Covered Bridges*
*Images of Patrick County: Postcards*
*Images of Patrick County*
*Ararat River Scenes*
*Never Forget: Patrick and Henry Counties in Vietnam*
*Upward Toil: The Lester Family of Henry County Virginia*
*Martinsville, Virginia*
*Henry County Heritage Book Volume One*
*Fieldale, Virginia*
*Bassett Virginia*
*Bassett Heritage Notes*
*"If Thee Must Fight, Fight Well:" William J. Palmer*
*George Stoneman's 1865 Raid*
*Beyond Mayberry: A Memoir of Andy Griffith and Mount Airy NC*
*Mount Airy, North Carolina*
*Civil War Stories From Mount Airy and Surry County North Carolina*
*A Dinky Railroad: The Mount Airy and Eastern Railway*
*Rangeley Virginia*
*The Graham Mansion: A History*
*Ghosts of the Graham Mansion*
*Stranger Than Fiction: Reid Stanger Fulton of the Graham Mansion*
*"Dear Phil:" Letters to and from Philmore G. Minter*
*Extraordinary Service: The Life and Military Heritage of David Minter*
*From Spencer Penn to Rives Road*
*Murder in a Rear View Mirror: Stories of True Crime*
*The Sweet Smell of Rain: A Father and a Daughter*
*Unreconstructed: Jubal Early and Franklin County Virginia*
*Ally's Cat: A Day in the Life of Abby Snyder*
*"Call The Shapes From The Mist:" Thirty Years of Speeches*
*Sweet Tea and Other Writings*
*Makers of History: Journeys Through African-American History*

# The Strange Case of Not Adams

Mama's Grandfather

Arson, Power, and Politics in Civil War Era Patrick County Virginia

By Thomas D. Perry

Patrick County Virginia History Series

## Tom Perry's
## Laurel Hill Publishing

**Thomas D. "Tom" Perry**
4443 Ararat Highway
P O Box 11
Ararat VA 24053

276-692-5300
laurelhillpub@gmail.com
https://squareup.com/store/
laurel-hill-publishing-llc

Autographed copies available at  https://squareup.com/store/laurel-hill-publishing-llc
and
Available Tom Perry's Author Page on Amazon at https://www.amazon.com/-/e/B002F4UJGEA

AUTOGRAPHED COPIES OF TOM PERRY'S BOOKS AVAILABLE ONLINE E

https://squareup.com/store/laurel-hill-publishing-llc

PAPERBACK AND KINDLE VERSIONS AVAILABLE ONLINE FROM AMAZON

https://www.amazon.com/-/e/B002F4UJGE

**ISBN:** 9798840193235

For Adrienne and Autumn

Mama's Grandfather
N P Adams

**Notley Price Adams**

# Contents

Nottey P. Adams, charged with setting fire to, and burning the house of Col. Jefferson T. Lawson, in Patrick county, Va., has been sent on to the Circuit Court of that county, for trial.

# PART ONE

## ARSON

## Chapter One

## *"A Most Litigious Man"*

Notley Price Adams comes down to us as a man who liked to stir things up. Before the famous crime, this book describes, Adams had a long history in Patrick County, Virginia, for finding himself involved in court cases. The Order Books in the Patrick County Court House have multiple mentions of these actions, especially Order Books #8, #9, and #11, including bad blood between Notley P. Adams and Jefferson T. Lawson and his brother, Madison T. Lawson, in July 1858. Adams was involved in a case against Benjamin Weddle a month later, in August 1858.

Adams lived six miles from Lawson in 1859 and thirteen miles from the courthouse in Taylorsville, now Stuart, Virginia. Although I seldom see it called by that name. It is usually described as Patrick Court House. Adams lived on 99 acres along the Smith River, valued at $800 in 1859.

On September 11, 2001, I was in the Library of Virginia researching Civil War General James Ewell Brown "Jeb" Stuart in the Special Collections Department. Governor John Letcher was a cousin of Stuart, and I was looking through Letcher's papers. I did not know about the terrorist attacks until noon when I came up for air upon hearing two of the staff discussing it.

I came across this entry in Virginia's Civil War Governor's papers. "An important function of the governor was issuing reprieves and pardons. Copies of court cases, clippings, petitions, and correspondence supplement the pardons. The pardon papers are filed separately in the chronological series at the end of each month. One significant pardon involved the case of Notley P. Adams of Patrick County, who was charged with arson. Letcher pardoned Adams in December 1863, after serving three years in the penitentiary. A map of the area in Patrick County where the crime was committed is included in the papers. The governor also received and issued proclamations and requisitions regarding escaped convicts and fugitives."

I had never heard of Notley P. Adams before that day, so I requested to see the materials. They arrived in three large folders, including over four hundred individual sheets documenting the pardon request by Adams to Governor Letcher.

Since twenty years ago, the Library of Virginia has microfilmed the whole collection, and you can scan the documents into pdf files; that is what I did in the fall of 2019. That has led to this book with easier access to this case about my home county of Patrick in far southwest Virginia.

In Virginia, Patrick County likes to put biblical names on places. Ararat for the "Mountains of Ararat," where Noah's Ark landed in the book of Genesis in the Old Testament. The Dan River comes from Dan, the fifth son of Jacob, which is related to judgment. Dan was the founder of the Tribe of Dan, the second largest tribe of Israelites. Among his descendants was Samson.

The community of Meadows of Dan in Patrick County applies a romantic name to the land drained by the Dan River. Just before the War Between The States erupted in 1861, one man was accused of arson. In April 1859, Notley Price Adams was accused of burning the vacant home of Jefferson T. Lawson near the Patrick and Floyd county lines near the Dan River and the Laurel Fork.

Local tradition says Notley Price Adams stood before the judge and was asked to state his name. "Not Adams," he replied. The aggravated judge said, "Well, then who are you," which he heard again, "Not Adams." The exasperated judge stated, "Well if you are not Adams, who are you?" The question reverberates down to us today.

This book tells the story of Adams and the times he lived in Patrick County, Virginia, where the more things change, the more they stay the same. When a small clique of people in the county seat tries to destroy a man using trumped up evidence to convict him of a crime. This story is set in the War Between The States when Virginia tried to leave the Union. Patrick County would leave Virginia if it did not secede and become The Free State of Patrick.

Notley Price Adams was the son of William Adams alias Price. Notley was considered a "bastard" because he was born before William married Nancy Ramey in 1801. Family tradition holds that William was cut out of his own father's will because of disobedience. He left home and changed his name.

Notley married Celia Akers on December 11, 1823. Their children, including Isaac (1824-1905), Alaminta (1827-1907), married Gabriel Bowling, Elizabeth (1829-1908) married John Lee, John (1831), Exonie (1832) married George Lansay, Adaline (1837) married James Taylor, Stalina (1838) married William Taylor, Jathina (1840-1910), and Nathaniel (1842-1864). The latter was killed at Winchester during the Civil War.

In the 1850 Census, Notley is listed as 49 years old and Celia age 43. Before the arson case, Notley was sued for slander and sent to prison. A local doctor had an affair, and Adams told about it even though he maintained his innocence.

Nine years later, the Patrick County Land Book #8 lists Adams owning 2,111 acres worth $1,415. He owned 400 acres in Rock Castle Gorge, 489 acres in Tuggle's Gap, 364 acres near Mabry's Mill, 108 acres near Meadows of Dan, and over 850 acres along the Smith River.

At the same time, Jefferson Lawson owned 200 acres worth $100, and his brother, Madison, owned 150 acres worth $100.

During the time of the court case detailed in this book, Adams found himself in debt to many such as $500 to Staples and Wade using John Adams, a slave, as security.

Over the years, Notley conveyed the property to his children to avoid using the land to pay debts. Fraudulently using children often caused the creditors to request the deeds be null and void.

# Chapter Two

## Fire In The Night

L. G. Rucker deposed Anna Connor on June 2, 1859.

Connor said she saw a light pass her house on the Conner Spur

Road as rain fell between 8 and 9 pm on Friday, April 29, 1859. in

Meadows of Dan, Patrick County, Virginia. She said it was Notley

Price Adams traveling toward Conner Spur Road.

James A. Ingram did not see Adams on his way to the store

that day, but it was a dark night, and Ingram did not see anyone

that evening. Isaac Jones was burning logs that Friday with Sally

Hill and her daughter, and they remembered hearing someone or

something make a noise nearby.

At the same time, a "dwelling house" worth $100 that was

not finished or occupied but had property inside valued at $500

belonging to Jefferson Turner Lawson was the victim of arson.

Jefferson bought the property, 200 acres, from his father, William

Lawson, for $200 on February 23, 1853, recorded in Patrick

County Deed Book 14 on page 343, located 17 miles from the

courthouse near the Floyd/Patrick County lines along the Dan River.

William Lawson, born in 1802, married Anna Thompson and had a dozen children. Their first son, Madison J. Lawson, was born in 1827. The second son was Jefferson T. Lawson. Jefferson Lawson was gone from Wednesday until Saturday evening when the house was burnt. He went to the structure on Sunday morning.

On May 23, 1859, Madison L. Lawson stated that since it was too dark to examine the night of the fire, he waited until the next morning, Saturday, to travel to the courthouse, Patrick Court House, or Taylorsville as it was known, to tell his brother, Jefferson T. Lawson about the fire. Madison stated that a horse had been tied to the corner of a fence near a spring near the house that was secluded with a private path of sixty to seventy paces from the new road by John DeHart. Madison said he followed the tracks on Sunday, and they went up the mountain following a road to Floyd Court House.

Suspicion quickly centered on Notley P. Adams, and he was arrested on Monday morning for several reasons, such as a "matching switch" off a bush near where the horse was tied, and the horseshoe tracks matched Notley Adams' horse. In a May 31, 1859, deposition, Preston Cooke said he heard Adams offered $10 to get a man to do them (The Lawsons) as much private injury as possible. Adams said the Lawsons were trying to "break him up." Adams indicated to Cooke that he wanted to injure the Lawsons himself. John Crews and David Layman witnessed Adams offering the $10.

The bad feelings were returned as Moses Hylton said in a deposition that William Lawson, the father of Jefferson T. Lawson, told him that he hated Adams. Adams went to jail from May 23 until June 8, 1859, with no bail. In July, Judge Fulton granted $1000 bail after a Writ of Habeas Corpus was filed.

Depositions of what seemed like everyone in Patrick County began. From the depositions, the case was hampered by a strange spring snow storm the next morning, Saturday, as the strange weather event obscured the tracks that seemed important.

On May 31, James A. Ingram was deposed and stated that he went to Adam's store to get a shroud for Jacob Hylton's wife. Ingram stated that Mrs. Adams helped him. Ingram went by Connor's Mill, Bowling's Mill, and Kendrick's Spur by Richardson's to the top of the mountain arriving home at 10 pm and stating he saw no one.

Jefferson Lawson refused to compare Adam's horseshoe with the tracks saying he thought Adams had another route. William Turner stated that Colonel Stuart Hanby on a mule and Rufus Turner on a horse tried to reenact Adams' route and left no tracks.

On June 1, Isaac Jones stated he was burning logs with two men and heard voices but was unsure of the direction. He stated he often saw Adams on Connor's Spur Road.

On June 4, Samuel A. Motley stated that he met William Burwell, John S. Adams, Gabriel Bowling, James Taylor, James Ingram, Rufus Woolwine, John Elgin, Robert Terry, and William Lewis at the Round Meadows on the Thursday after the arson. The tracks in question went in the direction of Kendrick's Spur. The horse shoe was a match with two notches and is in possession of James Ingram. They checked the Langhorne yard for tracks and found none.

On June 7, L. G. Rucker, Deputy Clerk of Patrick County, deposed James Langhorne, who stated that William Burwell visited his house. It then snowed. Burwell left, leaving the track on the gravel, which could not have lasted long.

On June 8, 1859, Adams was remanded for trial, and bail was refused. The next day James Moir received $70 for taking testimony. That same day, Moses Hylton stated he heard William Lee say he hated the prisoner, Adams, so bad that he never intended to try any case he was involved in. Three of Lee's neighbors swore that Adams could not get a fair trial due to Lee's bad feelings toward him.

Jefferson T. Lawson

# Chapter Three

## Court

In September 1859, a grand jury sat to hear evidence.

James Shelton
W. C. Potter
William D. Smith
William Lemon
Moses Hylton
James Dalton
G. B. Lanclefor
Harris Cloud
John H. Burnett
Warren Mogney
Benjamin Weddell
John L. Anglin

Those who gave evidence were the following.

Preston Cox
John Cruise
John C. DeHart
Jefferson T. Lawson
Madison Lawson
William Lawson
William Lee
Henry Richardson
Randolph Shelor
John Walker

"Having received their charge, the jury withdrew and after some time returned into Court and presented an indictment for felonious and malicious house burning." Defense counsel moved for a change of venue. The court was dismissed and continued the next day at 10 am. Adams was remanded to jail. The following day the change of venue motion was denied, and the trial continued to the next term set to begin on April 12, 1860. Adams received bail of $1000 with "two securities" put up by Gabriel Bowing and John Lee with a penalty of the same amount of $1000.

On September 8, 1859, Robert DeHart and John Boyd swore under oath that Adams could not get a fair trial. Patrick County Circuit Court indicted Adams on September 13, 1859, for "Feloniously and Maliciously" burning down a structure. A motion for a change of venue was overruled. Bail of $2,000 was extended until the next term. On September 16, 1859, Adams swore under oath before John C. Clark that he could not get a fair trial.

On April 12, 1860, Adams pled not guilty, but twenty-four jurors could not be conveyed, and the court was continued the next day. On April 13, 1860, a panel of twenty-four jurors sat. The defense struck eight from the pool. The jury included the following.

Seth Barber
William Deatherage
Abram Dillion
George Frans
William McMillian
Isaac Martin
Braxton Perdue
John Rucker
Abel Trent
Fieldale Trent
William Wimbush
John Yates


Adams pled not guilty. Deputy Sheriffs present were John R. Gilbert and Hardin Moore. The trial adjourned until the next day, Saturday, April 14, 1860, when evidence was heard, and again on Monday, April 16, starting at 9 am, and again on April 17, 18, and 19.  On April 19, the jury could not agree on a verdict, a "hung jury, "and Adams was remanded to jail. That same day, April 19, Jacob Hylton failed to appear for the defendant after being subpoenaed. He appeared the next day, April 20. Another change of venue was overruled, and bail was denied.

Jury members included the following.

William Wimbush
William McMillian
William Deatherage
Abram Dillon
? Trent
Braxton Perdue
John Yates
George Frans
John Rucker
Isaac Martin
Seth Barber


Deputies at the trial were John Gilbert and Hardin Moore. Rufus Turner was Sheriff of Patrick County.

On June 22, 1860, Judge George Gilmer of Patrick County held a special term to begin on June 10. Jurors were summoned from Franklin and Henry counties. A guilty verdict came down four days later, and Adams was sentenced to three years. The verdict was set aside, and a new trial was awarded.

In July 1860, a second trial began in Henry County, Virginia, where Adams was convicted. Politicians like to see their names on things, including counties. Patrick Henry, the first non-

British Governor of Virginia, could see his name on a map forever more.

Jury members included the following.

James Wade
Eli Davis
Newson Pace
John Hutchenson
Silas Marsterjo
Daniel Shumate
John Edwards
Edward Wade
Lewis Stone
W. B. Heptenstall
Alexander Ferguson
W. C. Barber


The jury found Adams guilty and sentenced him to three years in prison, but Judge Andrew Fulton overturned the verdict because he felt the testimony was insufficient. Fulton stated in 1863 that he felt a "slight suspicion of his guilt. The prejudice against him on the part of the prosecution and his friends was very great…and would not have suffered a conviction in my court upon the testimony." Adams was remanded to jail on July 11, 1860.

On August 24, 1860, the case was brought before Carroll County Circuit Court with a Writ of Habeas Corpus. Physician William Taylor said that the prisoner, Notley Price Adams, had disease including an excessive flow of urine, which was "greatly reducing him" Diabetes was mentioned, and that confinement caused the disease along with mental excitement. "The jail of Patrick County is unhealthy." It was a place conducive to typhoid fever, not well ventilated, and a filthy place with rotten timber and small damp cells.

Judge Fulton issued a court order demanding that a public official deliver an imprisoned individual to court to show a valid reason for personal detention. Adams got a $1500 bail with security guaranteed by William Burwell and A. M. Lybrook. On September 10, 1860, Adams swore before Judge Gilmer that he could not get a fair trial. Testimony from a doctor said that Adams' confinement would damage his health.

September 10 saw another Special Term of Court with a change of venue accepted and moved to Henry County, Virginia, and bail was refused.

On September 13, 1860, a grand jury convened at the Patrick County Courthouse with William P. Floyd as foreman. The trial venue was changed to Henry County, and bail was denied. Patrick County attorneys for Adams were W. A. Burwell, Nat Shelton, James Whittle, R. Stapes, and A. M. Crock.

The jury included the following.

Joseph Brim
Ewell J. Conner
Joseph Edwards
David Hall
Joseph Hall
James Harbour
Henry Rea
Fleming Reynolds
James Richardson
Thomas Shelton
Marshall Smith
A.J. Spencer
William Spencer
William Tatum
Samuel Terry
Linville Walker
John Willis, Sr.

Hiram Wright

Witnesses against Adams include the following.

Madison Lawson
Preston Cook
Henry Bowling
William Black
William Turner
Henry Webb
Merabeau Turner
Henry Richardson
Tazwell Turner
Jefferson T. Lawson
Andrew Bowling
Jonathan DeHart
James Richardson
William Thompson
Peter Cruise
Elizabeth Hylton
Sarah Hylton
William Lee
William Lawson
John DeHart
Randolph Shelor
Claiborne Lawson
J. H. DeHart
Creed Williams
Elizabeth Williams
John C. DeHart
John Cockerham

On September 8, John Bird and Robert DeHart indicated

they did not believe Adams could not get a fair trial. They were not alone in that feeling. On September 12, James A. Fulton, G. W. Wigginton, and William Smith On September 16, 1859, John C. Clark stated that he did not believe that Adams could get a fair trial saying that "prejudice existing against him on the part of many influential men in this county including the sheriff's son Crawford Turner influenced the jury."

On July 8, 1862, in Henry County Court, another change of venue was requested to Floyd County and denied. A special term of the court began in Henry County.

Jurors chosen on September 16, 1862, included

William Abingdon
Harman Edwards
Dandridge Harris
John Jameson
John Jones
Frederick Morris
John Morris
Anderson Purdy
Matthew Seay
Charles Stockton
George Thompson
Iredell Wray

On July 17, 1862, the case went to Henry County Circuit Court. The case began at 8:15 am. Two days September 19, 1862, later, the jury could not agree on a verdict resulting in another "hung jury." John Morris withdrew from the jury. Bail was set at $5,000 with security guaranteed by William Burwell, Gabriel Bowling, Moses Hylton, and James Taylor. Judge Gilmer felt the testimony was insufficient, like Judge Fulton.

The next day Judge Fulkerson set aside the verdict, feeling that the evidence did not justify the verdict. The prosecutor was not elected to try the case in Henry County, and Adams was granted a new trial.

The next day Judge Fulkerson set aside the verdict, feeling that the evidence did not justify the verdict. The prosecutor was not elected to try the case in Henry County, and Adams was granted a new trial.

Every July, Notley broke out of jail. The Patrick County Order Book #8 lists him indicted for escaping from jail on July 28, 1862, and a year later to the day on the same charge.

April 1, 1863, saw the case continued in Henry County until the next term with a bail of $5,000 and a continuance. Lawyers for Adams in Henry County were J. M. Whittle, Hugh Dillard, and

William Treadway. William Burwell, Gabriel Bowling, Moses Hylton, and James Taylor guaranteed bail security.

On September 1, 1863, a jury including Thomas Davis, Benjamin Cahill, Brice Hollandsworth, James Hollandsworth, Pleasant Nance, John Motley, Andrew Wilson, George Tusk, David Covington, William Bullington, Riley Newman, and William Mills.

On September 3, the jury found Adams guilty and sentenced him to three years in prison. A motion for a new trial was denied.

On September 3, 1863, a fourth trial in Henry County resulted in Adams's conviction for "felonious house burning" and a sentence of three years. Judge Wingfield believed Adams to be guilty.

Adams asked for the verdict to be set aside as he was not prosecuted by an attorney elected to prosecute in the county. William Martin and Christopher Thomas conducted the prosecution, with the latter representing William Lawson and the former representing Jefferson Lawson. John Wooten was the

Henry County attorney representing Adams. They again called for a change of venue.

On September 5, Adams was sent to the penitentiary in Richmond. "The Sheriff being apprehensive that the prisoner might escape."

Rufus James Woolwine was one of the many people deposed in the case of Notley Price Adams in 1859. The following pages show the actual transcription in the Library of Virginia and a transcript of the original.

Commonwealth
vs
A P Adams          3. day of June 1859.

Rufus I Morton    witness for defendant. sworn says.
                        on Thursday I went to
the Round Meadows, there in company with Wm H
Barnwell, Jno A Taylor, Gabriel Boling, Jno A Ingram,
Jno A Motley. John Elgin, William Lewis, Robert
A Terry. we there discussed to whilst we were
there Claiborne Dehart came by.   This shoe
now shown me, looks like the shoe that came off of
the right fore foot of Mr Barnwells horse.
We had been applying this shoe to tracks near
the crab apple bush. —      John C Dehart showed
us a track, he took this same shoe. and placed
it in a track, I was standing by, it filled the
track as well as could be expected, it turned on a root.
that near the stump & crab apple bush I noticed
six tracks that corresponded with the shoe of Mr
Barnwells we had applied — in the path leading to Kenricks Har.
Jeff T Lawson came by the crab apple bush whilst
we were at that point, he got down and
examined the tracks near the crab apple bush &
stump. I did not hear him say anything about
the tracks that I recollect.
the track that I saw John C Dehart apply the
shoe in, was in the path that leads to Kend-
ricks there. between the stump and crab apple
bush., where a part of the track rested on
a root.      The shoe filled as well as could
be expected, from the way it filled over the
root..
The next point we went to, was between the

crab apple bush & the Widow Dsharks.
We found a track where the horse left the road
& came back into the road that lead to
Kenricks Spur, the shoe was applied
to the track. There had been rain on the
track, it fitted tolerable well. We could not
tell whether it was the shoe that made
the track or not.

I went to the Widow Dsharks, I saw John R
Walker, ~~Jno~~ Dshart, John ~~R~~ Dshart
I requested John Dshart to go with us and
show us the track he had been pursuing.
He did not go. He refused to go.

John R Walker went back with me & showed
me a track betwixt the crab apple tree &
the Widow Dsharks; this was before we
applied the shoe to the track.

We went on to the black smith shop of Jas
Langhorne; and the right hind shoe of the horse
of Mr Barwell was taken off.— The shoe
taken off at this place was put in the possession
of William Lewis.

We made examination around the tree, the
place for tying horse's at Mr J.S. Langhornes
and found no distinct tracks.

We went on to near R.T. Shelor's and at that
place Mr Jno.T Earhart came to us.—
(John C Dshart left us at the ~~road~~ apple bush.
Jno Elgin Lett T.Lawsons, left us at the Widow Dsharts;)
after Mr Barwell returned from R T Shelors we
went on to the track around Jno Dshart's fence.
R T Shelor did not return with Mr Barwell —

We applied the shoes of Mr Barwell to several tracks at the blind path around Mrs Dehart's fence. The shoes fit very well, as well as could be expected. There had been rain on the tracks.

The tracks around the blind path made by the fore shoes were made by swelled heels. The tracks made by the hind shoes had the appearance of of being made by corkd heels. We could not tell exactly, it had rained on the tracks, but fitted very well.

We went on from this blind path, beyond where the house was burnt; near a spring, the shoe was applied to tracks there, and fitted as they did at the blind path.

In the corner of the fence, it had all the appearance of a horse being leed there, I saw no tracks, that plain enough to measure or apply the shoes to.

That the place where the horse appeared to be tied in the corner of the fence were much fresher than the tracks, no measured in the blind path. and had the appearance of not having had any rain on them.

I that in the corner of the fence, I saw an impression of a track, that appeared to be not shod or smoothly shod

I saw another track along the blind path. it was a great deal fresher, than the one we measured & applied the shoes to. It had the appearance of not having had any rain on it and appeared to have rode on the out side of the path excervising the other track. It had

the appearance of not being shed behind
except there two tracks. I saw no other tracks in
the blind path that I recollect of.

Jas A. Ingrum & John Elgin had measures that I
suppose to be the same measures. I saw them
take of their horses shoes, at Bowling Mill.

I saw a track, at a stump, betwixt John DHs
and the creek. Mr Barwell applied the
shoe to the track, which apparently had
floundered over the stump. my attention
was called to how the shoe fitted, it fitted
very well.

Mr Barwell took a stick, and run it through the
nail hole and it appeared to fit the impression
supposed to be made by a nail.

This was on the first day.

Betwixt the road coming from Rt Shelors and the forks of the road near
the new school house; we were shewn a track
by John Elgin, the hind shoes of Mr Burwell
were applied to the track, and they did not fit.

The print of a stick was there, where this track
had been measured previously. This track
at this place was going in the direction of
the burnt house. This was on the first day.

On Friday morning, Semarcus Lewis, William
Lewis, Robert Henry, Wm Burwell, John T
Earhart, & my self. we came to the Crab apple
tree, to the track we had examined on Thursday
I saw the shoe applied, the right near shoe of Mr Burwell
to the tracks at the crab apple tree; but did
not pay attention enough to it to say, whether
it fit or not.

37

Between the midway Dshart and the forks of the
road near the new school house, we met with
John CDShart, Mr Barwell invited him to
turn back with us, he did so.    He showed us
a track which appeared to have left the Floyd Ct.
road, passing through <ins>into the road leading</ins> approx, in the direction of the
burnt house, the track shown us by John CDShat
appeared to be barefoot behind, and therefore I
paid no farther attention to it.

This track did not correspond at all with the
track we measured at the blind path, and at the
Lound meadows.

From the forks of the road near the new School
house, to the cross road near the Shelor place.
I saw no tracks that appeared to be made by
the shoes of Mr Barwell, & there no tracks corresp-
-onding with tracks that I saw made by the
horse of the prisoner at Bowling mills.

From the cross road, near Rarford
the Shelor place, to Rarford, a situate level
opposite Wm Hylton's field. I saw a track
corresponding in appearance with the track
of the prisoners horse made at Bowling mills,
Mt Rarford.   Mr Rarford shewed us a track,
I thereto the measure of a he, a supeman
was applied, and it fitted as well as could
be expected —    Here Rarford & Ira Hylton
joined us, & we went on down in the direction of the cross road, near the Shelor place.
We went into Ira Hylton's new ground. I
paid no attention to the measurement or
examination at this place.

~~going toward the upper~~
~~Cabin brought~~

Mr Robert a Terry took a measure from the shoes of the mare, and they were applied to tracks in the path leading toward the upper Cabin, the tracks were both going & returning the measure taken from the mares shoe by Mr Terry fitted these tracks very well. We came from this point to the cross roads near the Shelor place, and took the road leading toward Connors Spur, we came on down the Connors Spur road to a field. I saw Ingrum measured applied to these tracks, and the meas. are fit very well.

I saw other tracks in the Connors Spur road that corresponded nearer with the tracks at Raiford, than they did with the tracks at the blind path near John D Shack. though I took no particular notice of the tracks except the one I saw measured at the field. I saw no track between the round meadows and the forks of the road near the new School house. That I saw measured, that corresponded with the tracks of the prisoners horse made at Bowling mill.

Rufus J. Woolwine

Commonwealth of Virginia v. Notley P. Adams

Taken in open court on the 3<sup>rd</sup> of June 1859 by L. G. Rucker

Depositions of Rufus James Woolwine, witness for defendant, sworn says

"On Thursday, I went to the Round Meadows. There is company with William A. Burwell, James Taylor, Gabriel Boling, James Ingram, Samuel Motley, John Elgin, William Lewis, Robert Terry, whilst we were there Claiborne Dehart came by.

This shoe now shown me, look like the shoe that came off of the right forefront of William Burwell's horse. We had been applying this shoe to tracks near the crab apple bush. John C. Dehart showed us a track. I was standing by it filled the track as well as could be expected, it turned over a root that near the stump and crab apple bush I noticed no other tracks that corresponded with the shoe of Mr. Burwell's, we had applied except the one I saw in the leading to Kendrick's Spur.

Jeff T. Lawson came by the crab apple bush whilst we were at that point, he got down and examined the track near the crab apple bush and stump. I did not hear him say anything about the tracks that I recalled.

The tracks that I saw John C. Dehart apply the shoe in, was between the stum and crab apple bush, where a part of the track rested on a root. The shoe filled as well as could be expected from the way it fille over the root.

The next point we went to, was between the crab apple bush and the Widow Dehart. We found a track where the horse left the road that led to Kendrick's Spur. The shoe was applied to the track there had been rained on the track. It fitted tolerable well. I could not tell whether it was the shoe that made the track or not.

I went to the Widow Dehart's. I saw John R. Walker, William Dehart, John Dehart. I requested John Dehart to go with us and show us the track he had been pursuing. He did not go. He refused to go. John R. Walker went back with me and showed me a track betwixt the crab apple track and the Widow Dehart. This was before we applied the shoe to the track.

We went on to the blacksmith shop of James Langhorne, and the right hind shoe of the horse of William Burwell was taken off. The shoe was taken off as the place was put in the possession of William Lewis.

We made examination around the tree, the placed for tying horses at W, J. S. Langhorne's, and found no distinct tracks.

We went on to near R. T. Shelor's, and at that place, William John Earhart came to us. John C. Dehart left us at the road at the crab apple bush. John Elgin, Jeff T. Lawson, left us at the Widow Dehart's after William Burwell returned from R. T. Shelor's. We went on to the path around the John Dehart fence. R. T. Shelor did not return with William Burwell.

We applied this shoe of William Burwell to several tracks at this blind oath around Joh Dehart's fence. The shoes fit very well, and as well as could be expected. There had been rain on the tracks.

The tracks around the blind path made by the fore shoes were made by swelled pads. The tracks made by the hind shoes had the appearance of being made by cork heels. I could not tell exactly. It had rained on the tracks but fitted very well.

We went on from this blind path, beyond where the house was burnt, near a spring. The shoe was applied to tracks there and fitted as they did at the blind path.

In the corner of the fence, it had all the appearance of a horse being tied there. I saw no tracks that are plain enough to measure or apply the shoes too. That place where the horse appeared to be tied in the corner of the fence were much fresher than the tracks we measured in the blond path and had the appearance of not having had any rain on them.

That is the side of the road near the corner of the fence. I saw an impression of a track that appeared to be not shod or shoddily shod.

I saw another track along the blind path. It was a great deal fresher than the one we measured and applied the shoes to. It had the appearance of not having had any rain on it and appeared to have rode on the outside of the path, examining the other track. It had the appearance of not being shod behind except there two tracks. I saw no other tracks in the blind path that I recollect.

James A. Ingram and John Elgin had measures that I suppose to be the same measure. I saw them take off the kinsman's horse shoes at Boling's Mill. I saw a track, at a stump, betwixt John Dehart's and the creek. William Burwell applied the shoe to the tracks, which apparently had blundered over the stump. Attention was called to him the shoe fitted. It fitted very well.

William Burwell took a stick and run it through the mail hole, and it appeared to fit the impression supposed the be made by a nail.

This was on the first day.

Betwixt the road crossing R.T. Shelor's and the forks of the road near the new school house, we were shown a track by John Elgin, the kind of shoes of William Burwell were applied to the track, and they did not fit.

The front of a stick was there, where this track had been measured previously. This track was this place was going in the direction of the burnt house. This was on the first day.

On Friday morning, Demarcus Lewis, William Lewis, Robert A. Terry, William A. Burwell, John T. Earhart, and myself we came to the crab apple tree to the track we had examined on Thursday. I saw this shoe applied, the right hind shoe of William Burwell, to this track at the crab apple tree, but did not pay attention enough to it to say whether it fit or not.

Betwixt the Widow Dehart's and the forks of the road near the new school house, we met with John C. Dehart, William Burwell, invited him to turn back with us, he did so.

He showed us a track which appeared to have left the Floyd Court House road passing through into the road leading in the direction of the burnt house. The track shown us by John C. Dehart appeared to be barefoot behind, and therefore I paid no further attention to it.

The track did not correspond at all with the track we measured at the blind path, and at the Round Meadow.

From the forks of the road near the new school house to the crossroads near the Shelor Place. I saw no track that appeared to be made by the shoes of William Burwell and not tracks corresponding with tracks that I saw made by the horse of the prisoner at Boling's Mill.

...crossroads near the Shelor Place to and in an opposite Ira Hylton's field, I saw a track corresponding in appearance with the track of the prisoner's horse made at Boling's Mill. H. Radford, W. Radford showed us a track, I think the measure of James A. Ingram was applied, and it fitted as well as could be expected. H. Radford and Ira Hylton joined us, and we went on down in the direction of the crossroads near the Shelor Place. We went into Ira Hylton's new ground. I paid no attention to the measurement or examination at this place.

Robert A. Terry took a measure from this shoe of the mare, and they were applied to the tracks in the path leading toward the … cabin. The tracks were both going and returning the measure taken from the mare's shoe by William Terry fitted these tracks very well. We came from this point to the crossroads near the Shelor Place and took the road leading toward Conner's Spur. We came on down the Conner's Spur Road to a field. I saw Ingram measured and applied to these tracks, and the measure fit very well.

I saw other tracks in the Conner Spur Road that corresponded nearer with the tracks at Radford than they did with the tracks at the blind path near John Dehart. I took no particular notice of the tracks except the one I saw measured at the field. I saw no track between the Round Meadows and the forks of the road near the new school house. That I saw measured that corresponded with the rack of the prisoner's horse made at Boling Mill."

Rufus J. Woolwine

# PART TWO

## WAR

David Lee Ross commanded a company from Patrick County in the 51st Virginia Infantry. *Courtesy of Paul Ross.*

# Chapter Four

## Patrick County's Civil War Soldiers

As Notley Price Adams made his way through multiple court cases in different jurisdictions, many of the people involved in his case found themselves involved in a bigger conflagration, the American Civil War. Among these was Jefferson T. Lawson, who owned the house Adams was accused of burning down.

Today the statue of a lone Confederate veteran shown on the cover of this book stands atop a large base erected in 1936 in front of the Patrick County Court House. Many people confuse this infantryman with the county's most famous soldier, James Ewell Brown "Jeb" Stuart, but Stuart's image adorns a plaque on the front of the base where you will read that he was born "near" the town that bears his name. In 1907, Richmond placed an equestrian statue of Stuart on Monument Avenue, and the base of it states that he was "Born in Patrick County, Virginia." He faces north, still symbolically keeping an eye out for invaders, protecting the city he gave his life defending.

The largest contribution of Patrick County to the war effort was the men serving in the armed forces of the Confederate States of America. Patrick men fought in all of the major engagements in Virginia, Maryland, Pennsylvania, Tennessee, Kentucky, and North Carolina. The majority of these men enlisted from Elamsville or Ararat at opposite ends of the county.

In April 1861, two militia companies, the 18th and the 156th provided some military training to Patrick's men. In the 1860 Census, 1617 men between the ages of 15 and 50 lived in Patrick County. Eighty-seven percent served in the war. These soldiers faced daunting odds in their service for the South. Seventeen percent became prisoners. Union soldiers wounded nine percent. Most horrifying for their families, twenty-seven percent made the ultimate sacrifice for Southern independence. At least 152 men from Patrick in the 42nd Virginia Infantry and only six at Appomattox. Of the 334 Patrick County residents who lost their lives in 1862, 102 died due to the war.

Patrick County men served in fifty different artillery, cavalry, and infantry regiments during the war. Twenty-five percent of them served in the 51st Virginia Infantry Regiment. The 50th, 24th, and 42nd Virginia Infantry Regiments contained the next largest numbers. Seven percent of Patrick Countians served in the cavalry and three percent in artillery units. Others served in diverse organizations such as the 5th Battalion Virginia Reserves, 6th Virginia Infantry, 58th Virginia Infantry, the Orange Artillery, and the 21st Virginia Cavalry. Many served in North Carolina units such as the 53rd Infantry Regiment or 2nd Cavalry Regiment.

The hardships endured in the army took a heavy toll on Patrick County's soldiers. Living in a somewhat secluded environment, they quickly contracted diseases such as measles, mumps, and smallpox, which many times proved fatal. Unsanitary living conditions caused many of them to come down with typhoid fever which, combined with pneumonia, was the most common cause of death.

Families sometimes came to the camps and took their loved one's bodies home for burial. Born on the Smith River in Patrick County, Jefferson Turner lived at the crest of the Blue Ridge Mountain in Floyd County before the war. He served in

Captain Sparrell Griffith's Company H, 54th Virginia Infantry.

Turner died of disease at Abingdon in May 1862. Family tradition

states his wife, Susan Short Turner, traveled by wagon to

Abingdon, brought his body back, and buried him at the head of

Shooting Creek, a journey of almost 300 miles.

The records indicate that half of all Patrick County soldiers

went "Absent Without Leave" (AWOL) one or more times during

the war. Officials listed large percentages as deserters. Some went

home to help with family problems. With most men away in the

army, often no one at home could plant or harvest the crops.

Fathers came home to see about them when wives and children

got sick.

In many cases, the soldiers returned to their units later.

Many records are incorrect because of poor record keeping and

the inability of company clerks to keep up with the men due to

hospitalization, capture, or transfer. If a man was not present at

roll call and the clerk did not know his whereabouts, he was listed

as "Absent Without Leave." Some companies did not attempt to

keep records near the end of the conflict. Toward the end of the war, some Patrick County soldiers took the Oath of Allegiance to the U.S. Government and "went North," with some joining the U. S. Army.

A company of infantry commanded by a captain and two lieutenants consisted of 100 men. On paper, a regiment contained ten companies with one thousand men commanded by a colonel. Ideally, a regiment had a lieutenant colonel, major, adjutant, quartermaster, surgeon, assistant surgeon, sergeant major, quartermaster sergeant, commissary sergeant, hospital stewards, and sometimes a band of musicians. While some companies and regiments started with the ideal numbers, very few maintained those numbers for very long. Desertions, illness, wounds, and deaths played havoc with manpower. Seldom did replacements fill all of the vacancies. For instance, at Antietam, Lee's regiments average 170 men. Most units ended the war with only a fraction of full strength.

A regiment served in a brigade with three other regiments, usually from the same state, commanded by a brigadier general. A brigade served as the basic tactical formation in battle and usually went by the name of its commander, such as the "Stonewall" Brigade. Two brigades made a division commanded by a major general. At least two divisions made up a corps commanded by a lieutenant general. An army made up of corps commanded by a general was the top unit in the Confederate hierarchy.

The chain of command for a Confederate private worked along these lines. In March 1865, Private George M. Agee served in Captain Rufus Woolwine's Company D, 51st Virginia Regiment of Infantry. Major William T. Akers commanded the 51st Virginia. The regiment was part of Wharton's Brigade, commanded by Major Peter J. Otey, in Wharton's Division, commanded by Brigadier General Gabriel C. Wharton. They belonged to the Second Corps led by Major General John B. Gordon in the Army of the Valley commanded by Lieutenant General Jubal A. Early, who reported to Secretary of War John C. Breckinridge, who served in the cabinet of Jefferson Davis, President of the Confederate States of America.

All of those who left Patrick in 1861 were volunteers. Enthusiastic speakers, often militia officers, organized meetings in several sections of the county. They made stirring speeches that resulted in hundreds of young men eagerly volunteering their services for repelling any invasion of the hated Yankee armies.

One of the first units organized in Patrick County was a company from the Spoon Creek area near Critz, which began enlisting men on May 22, 1861, and became Company H of the 42nd Virginia Infantry. Captain John Edmund Penn led this unit. The military tradition was strong in some families. Captain Penn descended from Colonel Abram Penn, commander of the area troops in the Battle of Guilford Courthouse during the American Revolution.

The first men from the "Free State of Patrick" to leave for war were ninety-eight men of Company I, 24th Virginia Infantry, under Captain A. M. Lybrook. Andrew Lybrook, an attorney, organized the unit at Patrick Court House. This company enlisted men on May 31, 1861.

On the north side of Bull Mountain, Captain David Lee Ross organized and trained a company on his farm near Elamsville. On June 14, 1861, he inducted a large number of volunteers that later became Company D, 51st Virginia Infantry Regiment. Captain Greenville (Granville) Conner organized a company on Smith River near the Jack's Creek Covered Bridge. This company became Company H, 51st Regiment of Infantry. More Patrick County men served in these two companies of this regiment than in any other outfit in the Army during the war.

In the far western section of the county, men joined a Carroll County company organized at Fancy Gap. Captain Alexander Haynes, a Patrick County native, commanded this unit that became Company E of the 29th Virginia Infantry.

In July 1861, Jefferson T. Lawson organized a company near Taylorsville that became Company K, 50th Virginia Infantry. At Patrick Court House on July 6, 1861, George H. Booker, a graduate of Randolph-Macon College and an Episcopal minister, organized and enlisted for one year and commanded the "Patrick County Grays," Company H, 58th Virginia Infantry Regiment.

A new reference book, Civil War High Commands, contains a section on the birthplaces of Confederate generals. The book credits Patrick County with J. E. B. Stuart, Alfred Cleon Moore, and Alexander Watkins Terrell.

Alfred Cleon Moore, born in Patrick County on December 12, 1805, moved to North Carolina as a boy. A physician and legislator in the "Old North State" at the outbreak of the Civil War, Moore returned to Virginia and, from April 17 until June 8, 1861, served as a brigadier general in the Provisional Army of Virginia. In November, he ranked as colonel of the 29th Virginia Infantry Regiment.

The 29th fought in Southwest Virginia and Kentucky, where in 1862, they fought future United States President James A. Garfield in the Battle of Middle Creek. The regiment transferred to Petersburg as Robert E. Lee's Army of Northern Virginia moved north into Maryland. Moore held the position of colonel until his resignation on April 8, 1863, due to "advanced age and failing health." He served in the reserves in Wythe County and continued as a physician after the war. Moore's mortal remains reside in the McGavoc Cemetery near Fort Chiswell, Virginia.

Born in Patrick County on November 3, 1827, Alexander Watkins Terrell moved to Missouri at age five. He attended the University of Missouri and moved to Texas in 1852, where he became a judge. Like his friend Sam Houston, Terrell opposed secession. In 1862, Terrell found himself a Captain in the First Texas Cavalry. He rose in rank to colonel by June 1863 in Terrell's Texas Cavalry Battalion.

The regiment fought in the Battle of Mansfield, Louisiana, along the Red River in April 1864. He commanded a brigade of three Texas cavalry regiments in September for seven months. On May 16, 1865, Edmund Kirby Smith promoted Terrell to brigadier general in the Trans-Mississippi Department, but the Confederate Senate did not confirm his appointment. Two days before his promotion, Terrell disbanded his regiment. In July, he fled to Mexico and became a colonel in the Mexican army for four months. He received a pardon from the United States in November 1865.

After the Civil War, Terrell practiced law and served in the Texas legislature with a stint under President Grover Cleveland as

United States Minister to Turkey from 1893 until 1897. Due to his work in the legislature on education, many consider him the "Father of the University of Texas." He wrote two books, one published in 1933 entitled From Texas to Mexico and the Court of Maximilian, and the second he co-edited in 1874 entitled Cases Argued and Decided in the Supreme Court of the State of Texas. He ran unsuccessfully for the United States Senate from Texas and served as the Texas Historical Association president. Alexander Terrell died in Mineral Wells, Texas, on September 9, 1912, and rests today in the state cemetery in Austin, Texas.

Many average Patrick Countians were Civil War soldiers, and Chief Justice of the U. S. Supreme Court Oliver W. Holmes said, "Touched by fire" during the war. The following are some of their stories.

James Gabriel Penn, born in 1845 at Penn's Store, served in the Corps of Keydets from the Virginia Military Institute at New Market in May 1864. He became a banker in Danville and the American Tobacco Company founder.

First Lieutenant Peter Washington Dalton of Company H, 42nd Virginia Infantry found himself a member of "The Immortal 600" in September 1864. A prisoner of the United States of America at Morris Island, South Carolina, Dalton lived under the fire of the Confederate guns at Charleston as a reaction to Union prisoners being treated similarly. While still a teenager in May 1861, Dalton enlisted from Ararat. Wounded at Kernstown in March 1862, hospitalized in July 1862 at Charlottesville with small pox, and a year later in Richmond with fever and captured at Spotsylvania Court House in May 1864, Dalton went to Fort Delaware for imprisonment. On August 20, 1864, Union officials transferred him to South Carolina, where they held him under fire as an "Immortal" from September 7 until October 21, 1864. Imprisoned at Fort Pulaski, Georgia, until November 21, then transferred to Hilton Head. Dalton returned to Fort Delaware on March 21, 1865.

For many, the war was a negative experience that left them bitter. Isaac Underwood enlisted in March 1862 in Company D, 12th Virginia Infantry, and proceeded to see just about every

Confederate hospital, including Petersburg, Williamsburg, Charlottesville, Richmond, and Lynchburg. He suffered from diseases such as typhoid, pneumonia, and smallpox but survived to desert in 1864 and lived to write his memoir: "I was forced to go into the War in sixty two... I stayed in the War until it closed, or rather, I stayed in the army and other places until it closed. I went North and stayed ten months in the winding up of the rebellion, for I was no war man anyway, and it was slaves that the issue was about, and I had none of these to fight for, and I thought it was wrong for me to fight for other people's property unless they paid me for it. This was one of the hardest trials of my life. To leave my wife and baby exposed to all the elements of danger at home, and myself plunged in the midst of cannons and swords and bullets, and all kinds of weather and camping out on the ground. Being very weakly, I soon became unable to do any service in camp at all, and was nearly always in the hospital. I there had typhoid fever, pneumonia, smallpox, and scrafulus [scrofulous], and was a burden to the hospital and myself, and a constant distress to my wife, fearing that I could never return home anymore."

Joshua Branch served in Company D, 51st Virginia Infantry, and Company K of the 140th Indiana Infantry. Born in Patrick County, Branch's enlistment papers describe him as a farmer, five foot nine inches in height at twenty-two years of age, with blue eyes, brown hair, and a dark complexion. He joined the Union army on October 6, 1864, and spent time at Murfreesboro, Tennessee, and then in the campaign to take Fort Fisher in North Carolina. He mustered out at Greensboro, North Carolina, in July 1865 and lived until 1907. Joshua Branch lies in the Pedigo Cemetery adjoining the J. E. B. Stuart's birthplace, Laurel Hill, in Ararat.

Others came to Patrick County after the war, such as James A. Grogan of Company D, 10th Alabama Infantry. His regiment was organized in Montgomery in June 1861 and fought at Dranesville with J. E. B. Stuart in December. The unit joined the Army of Northern Virginia in 1862, serving in Cadimus Wilcox's Brigade of Longstreet's, then A. P. Hill's Corps, until the surrender at Appomattox.

A headstone in the Hunter's Chapel Church Cemetery in Ararat lists James T. W. Clements of Pittsylvania County, 6th Virginia Cavalry. Sheridan's cavalry captured Clements and sixty men making a last stand at Yellow Tavern the day "Jeb" Stuart received his mortal wound on May 11, 1864. Present in Harrisonburg, Virginia, on June 6, 1862, Clements' company carried the dead Turner Ashby from the field. Clements served time in a Yankee prison before returning home to Virginia.

Andrew Jackson Stedman of Gates County, North Carolina, enlisted as a sergeant in Company B, 49th North Carolina Infantry, and received a wound at Malvern Hill in July 1862. He became a first lieutenant in the Signal Corps. He married Susan K. Staples of Patrick County after the war, practiced law in Stokes County, North Carolina, and edited the first newspaper in Patrick County, The Voice of the People, in 1876.

Finally, there is Samuel Granville Staples, the man from Patrick who voted on April 17, 1861, for secession at the state convention. The son of Abram Staples, he was born in Patrick County in 1821 and educated at Randolph-Macon, the University

63

of Virginia, and the College of William and Mary. Staples practiced law, served as Clerk of Circuit Court from 1844 to 1852, and was a member of the House of Delegates from 1852 to 1854. He served as a volunteer aide-de-camp for two months during the war to General J. E. B. Stuart in 1862 until he was discharged because of physical disabilities. Post-war, Staples served as a judge in the county for ten years and worked for the Department of the Interior in Washington, D. C. He lived until 1895.

Except for a raid by General Stoneman's Federal troops near the war's end, no Union forces entered Patrick County. Despite that, no war in history affected people's lives as the Civil War. As early as 1863, Virginia had passed a law for "Relief of Indigent Soldiers and Sailors," where each county would provide money and services. After the war in 1867, Virginia passed a law for artificial limbs. Virginia passed pension acts in 1888, 1900, and 1902 and noted in this book, along with disability claims.

The aftermath of the war had many effects on the women and children left behind. Survival became the main problem, and many applied for pensions. In 1915, Virginia covered funeral expenses for veterans and paid pensions from 1888, 1900, and 1902 once a year. Pensions varied from $180 for blindness and $78 for the loss of a limb to $43.20 for disability from disease. Matrons in Confederate hospitals received $48, and widow's pensions ranged from $30 to $48 depending on the time of death. Sarah Guynn began receiving $30.00 a year beginning in 1888 for her husband Levi of Company E, 29th Virginia Infantry. Family tradition states that the Carroll County Home Guard killed Levi, but Sarah's pension application states he died from a fever after he returned home in September 1863.

The pool of men of marriageable age forced many women to marry much older men, such as Edward Noah Martin, who was forty-eight years older than his bride, Naomi Caroline Moran. She kept a sense of humor, stating, "I'd rather be an old man's darling than a young man's slave."

Many children grew up never knowing their fathers, such as Susan Emma Moss, born after her father's death, Jesse Moss of Company G, 51st Virginia Infantry. Moss died of measles and rests today ten miles north of New Market in a cemetery near Mount

Jackson. His wife's pension application is the only record of his service in the Confederate Army.

Descendants of the veterans formed the Wharton-Stuart Camp of the Sons of Confederate Veterans on April 14, 1906, with George T. Munford as commandant, Samuel M. Lybrook as first lieutenant commandant, R. H. Dunkley as Second Lieutenant Commandant, R. E. Woolwine as Adjutant, L. C. Dickerson as a surgeon, John A. Adams as quartermaster, John W. Wimbush as chaplain, along with a treasurer, color sergeant, historian, and over seventy-six members.

Families discover parts of their past to this day. Mentoria Dehart Weaver lost her husband, Jesse Dehart, during the war. She married Daniel Weaver, and one of their children, Walter G. Weaver, designed Patrick County's two surviving wooden bridges, the Bob White and Jack's Creek in Woolwine. Jesse Dehart fought in Company A, 24th Virginia Infantry. As part of Pickett's Charge at Gettysburg in Kemper's Brigade, Dehart received a wound and faced capture and imprisonment. Exchanged in 1864, Jesse Dehart lost his life at Chafin's Farm near Petersburg. His recently discovered marked grave lies near George Pickett in Richmond's Hollywood Cemetery.

Patrick County's Civil War soldiers are all gone. They rest in graves from northern Georgia and Fort Donelson, Tennessee, to Finns Point, New Jersey, and Elmira, New York. The last veteran of the War, Joseph Henry Brown, served in Company G of the 24th Virginia Infantry. Born in 1843, he survived the war after being captured at Five Forks in April 1865, as Robert E. Lee's lines were broken around Richmond forcing the retreat that ended in surrender at Appomattox. Brown died in 1940 at 96, ending the last human link to the war.

**Rufus James Woolwine of the 51st Virginia Infantry wrote a memoir of his experiences during the war.**

*Courtesy of the Virginia Historical Society.*

## Chapter Five

## Rufus Woolwine and the 51st Virginia Infantry

In studying the Civil War, focusing on battles or leaders and forgetting about the ordinary infantry soldier is commonplace. In Patrick County, the same is true for James Ewell Brown "Jeb" Stuart. You see his name and image everywhere, but many infantry soldiers fought in the war and deserve recognition.

Rufus James Woolwine of the 51st Virginia Infantry Regiment saw many important places and events throughout the war. Not only did he live to tell about it, but he also kept notes during his time in the army. Immediately after the war, he compiled these notes (and probably hindsight) into a three-part diary. Mrs. Mabel Barksdale Norris, Woolwine's granddaughter, presented his papers to the Virginia Historical Society in 1962. She discovered the journal in a glass jar buried in an abandoned well during spring cleaning. Louis H. Manarin edited and published the diary in the Virginia Magazine of History and Biography in October 1963.

The Patrick County community of Woolwine gets its name from Rufus's father, the first postmaster, Thomas Woolwine. Sarah Adams Woolwine, his mother, was the daughter of Notley P. Adams. Rufus James Woolwine, born October 20, 1840, attended the common schools and went to work with his father as a saddler. He enlisted on June 14, 1861, as a private and mustered in as a fourth corporal on July 26.

According to all available records, at least 391 men from the county served in this unit. More Patrick Countians served in the 51st Regiment of Virginia Infantry than any other regiment. The companies from Patrick County were formed in June 1861. One group became Company C under David Lee Ross. Ninety-seven men drilled on his farm on present-day Highway 57 near the intersection with Pole Bridge Road. Captain Ross served as an officer in the county militia before the war. Other officers included William Tyler Akers, Abner J. Harbour, and Charles F. Ross, serving as lieutenants in Company C. After a few months, this company became Company D.

Another group called the "Blackhawk" company organized under Granville P. Conner at Davis Shop on the Smith River. Originally designated Company F, this unit became Company H with William G. Price, John M. Cruise, and Nathan B. Terry as lieutenants. Both companies drilled until July 24, 1861, then marched to Christiansburg, where they boarded a Virginia and Tennessee Railroad train for Wytheville. Augustus Forsberg wrote of them at this time, "It was interesting to notice the personnel of the volunteer-like mountaineers, they were courageous, fine physical development, and could compare with any troops on earth...Some in uniforms they had made at home, some with squirrel rifles, some with flint locks and bowie knives. Some had never seen a railroad. Once the sound of a locomotive was heard and the men acted like being shocked, one called out, 'She's a coming,' down went all guns and like a flock of sheep, ran down the hill to see the Iron Horse."

Born in Sweden in 1832, Forsberg served as a Swedish Army Engineer before coming to America in the 1850s. He rose to

Colonel and commanded the 51st Virginia Infantry Regiment in 1863.

Young men who were going off to war inspired Captain Ross' black servant, Britt, to poetry. Born in 1822 as a slave, Britt and a twin brother, Jordan, reportedly could not read or write.

"The twenty fourth of July, may long remember being,

The volunteers from Patrick the men to march away,

The patriotic spirit induces them to go,

To meet the Northern plunders and keep them from the shore.

A true hearted soldier he stands at his post,

In danger he's never found out of his course

He's willing to fight if it's five to their ten

Lord aid Captain Ross and all his brave men.

Lord aid our captain while we are in camp,

Grant every man to have oil in his lamp,

and be ready if called on with a load to depart,

with a beautiful beed on a northern man's heart.

Here's health to the poet that did make the song,

his life to be merry, his day's to be long,

good luck to all our soldiers that live under the sun,

success to Captain Ross and all his brave Patrick men."

After having dinner at Gabriel DeHart's home on Rock Castle Creek at the foot of Tuggle's Gap, Rufus Woolwine wrote in his diary on July 24, "The scene of parting is a day that can never be described, never be forgotten. Twas then we bid farewell to home, friends, and connections and took up the lines of march to meet the serried ranks of a strong but dastard foe. Twas then many of us looked upon our native soil as we thought for the last time." Upon arriving at Christiansburg, their accommodations caused Woolwine to write, "Landed there about one o'clock in the night and I do assure you that our feathers fell when they lighted us to our stall... What we were furnished with there overnight discouraged several so they laid in an excuse and plead for a discharge."

At Camp Jackson in Wytheville, they joined seven companies of the 51st Regiment of Virginia Infantry under the command of an 1847 graduate of the Virginia Military Institute and civil engineer, Gabriel C. Wharton. Men from all over southwest Virginia joined the regiment under "Old Gabe." Companies C and F from Patrick County joined their fellow Virginians, such as the "Wharton Grays," Company B from Wythe County under David P. Graham.

Other companies in the regiment included Company K, the "Bland Tigers," under Samuel Newberry, Company G, the "Floyd Gamecocks," under James W. Henley, and Companies A and D from Grayson County under Stephen M. Dickey and Ezekiel Young. Company B, the "Nelson County Rifles," under John T. Dillard and, Company E, the "Wythe Rifles," under William H. Cook, Company I contained men from Washington County under John P. Wolfe.

The last unit to join, Company L, hailed from Tazewell

County. The men listened to its eleven-piece regimental band. Burton Highley watched over the spiritual health of the men as minister of the regiment, and James Estill performed the duties of a regimental surgeon. The eleven companies came together due to Brigadier General John B. Floyd's need for troops in the Kanawha Valley in present-day West Virginia.

The men learned the hard lessons of war quickly. During their initial training, the troops received three days' rations. They ate all the rations at once and went hungry for two days. During the first year of the war, Woolwine "messed" or ate with N. C. Akers, J. F. Via, his brother D. G. Via, J. J. Vaughn, Tiller Thomas, and William Dennis Via until the reorganization of the regiment in 1862.

In August 1861, the regiment took the train to Bonsack Depot, just east of present-day Roanoke, and camped from August 5 until September 19. The regiment moved to the Kanawha Valley in present-day West Virginia in early September, leaving the two Patrick companies behind. The men from Patrick rejoined the regiment after about three weeks. An epidemic of measles broke out in the two Patrick companies. Two men, James Ross and Robert Hodges, from Company D, died from measles.

The 51st joined the 3rd Brigade in the Army of the Kanawha, participating in the Sewell Mountain Campaign. Robert E. Lee arrived on September 21 to take command. Rufus Woolwine and John T. Washburn heard Reverend G. S. Tuggle preach, and they slept in the pulpit the same night. Woolwine celebrated his birthday on October 20 at Raleigh Court House, noting," I enjoy our social activities, the association with ladies and gentlemen of like background, and the many warm friendships that have resulted, locally, and all over the south." Lee failed to meet his chief objective: preventing the Union forces from organizing these western counties into a new state. The Confederates lost control of the Kanawha Valley and retreated into the mountains. Disease, terrible weather, impassable roads, and lack of supplies, including weapons, food, and shelter, caused terrible hardships for the new troops resulting in death and desertion.

Woolwine traveled home to Patrick for one of his many visits during the war. On his return, the 51st transferred to take part in defense of Fort Donelson, Tennessee, in 1862. The regiment traveled to Bowling Green, Kentucky, to assist General Albert Sidney Johnston in his unsuccessful attempt to stop General Ulysses S. Grant. General John B. Floyd, a former governor of Virginia, commanded a division including the 51st.

The trip to the "Bluegrass State" took eight days for the regiment. The men traveled via five railroads to Bristol, Knoxville, Chattanooga, Nashville, and Bowling Green. During the Kentucky stay, Woolwine reported General Felix Zollicoffer's death at the Battle of Mill Springs on January 17, 1862, and his first pay: "Here we drawed the first money we ever drawed from the time we come into the service." James I. Robertson quotes General Floyd on the 51st in 1862, saying, "They have not a single dollar to purchase the least little comfort, even for the sick."

U. S. Grant earned the moniker "Unconditional Surrender"

when he forced Fort Henry's capitulation and Fort Donelson's capitulation. The 51st Virginia, under the command of another VMI graduate, Colonel James W. Massie, fought in the thick at Fort Donelson in February 1862. This battle was a rugged baptism into the rigors of war for the young Patrick Countians.

Rufus Woolwine wrote of the battle, "There we took a boat for Fort Donelson. Got there that night. On Wednesday the Twelfth of February we was marched out for fight. Worked all night throwing up breastworks. On the thirteenth, we lay in our ditches all day and such heavy cannonading was never heard before. That night it rained and we just had to lay in our ditches. Fourteenth, skirmishing along the line. Lay in our ditches that night. Fifteenth, just as day began to dawn upon the silvery waters of the Cumberland we engaged the enemy and drove him from his camp. When we succeeded in ascending the first hill such a sight my eyes never before beheld. Twas there I beheld the mangled dead and dying, laying in all imaginable forms. Yes, there several hundred miles from our native homes, and from those that was bound to us by the strongest ties of affection. I am happy to say that thanks to God Virginians done their duty as becomes true men and patriots. Though distantly situated, they thought of their happy homes far away that they was fighting for. With them as with all of Jeff's boys, they done all men could do."

On February 15, Wharton's Brigade attacked the Federal right and opened an escape route at the cost of nine killed, forty-three wounded, and five missing. The sniping generals, Floyd and Pillow, failed to follow up the success of the breakout. The next day Floyd's command escaped before the surrender of the fort. The men made their way to Nashville, Chattanooga, and finally to Abingdon. Going into winter camp at Glade Spring, the wounded recuperated in the hospital at Emory and Henry College.

The 51st continued in Wharton's Brigade in the Army of the Kanawha and remained in the Department of Southwestern Virginia through the rest of 1862. Captain David Lee Ross resigned from the company and returned to his farm at Elamsville. He assumed command of the county militia with the title of

Lieutenant Colonel. Later in the war, authorities inducted all militiamen into service. Ross then joined the 21st Virginia Cavalry Regiment.

At the beginning of the war, soldiers elected their officers. When the 51st reorganized in 1862, William Tyler Akers became captain of Company D. Woolwine received a promotion to Second Lieutenant. He went to work as an adjutant, purchasing supplies and salt and recruiting in the counties of Scott, Tazewell, and Patrick. Special duties, including recruitment, brought him home to Patrick County many times. During one of these visits, he arrested two "bushwhackers." Other duties included arresting men for making and selling liquor in Giles County in July 1862. He visited Patrick County in 1862 from May 5 through May 25, November 21 through December 12, and December 21 through the 28.

One of the principal objectives of the Union forces involved capturing the salt mines at Saltville and the lead mines in Wythe County. These threats required the Confederate government to keep forces in southwest Virginia to protect these sources. The mines were essential to the Confederate armies as the largest sources of both salt and lead were in southwest Virginia. In the spring of 1862, the 51st went to meet a Federal force that had captured Princeton. The regiment succeeded in driving the Federal forces from the nearly destroyed town.

A unit of the 51st under Captain William T. Akers traveled to White Sulphur Springs and lost to a stronger Federal force. Captain Akers and his troops escaped by burning a bridge behind them. In June 1862, the 51st returned to Giles County. Later that month, it encamped at Peterstown, now in West Virginia. On July 3, the unit assisted in defeating a Federal force at Mercer Courthouse. For the next several weeks, members of the 51st remained in camp near Narrows in Giles County.

In August 1862, General W. W. Loring assumed command of the Department of Southwestern Virginia. Wharton's Brigade (including the 51st and 50th Regiments and 23rd Battalion of Infantry along with Stamp's Artillery) moved into Monroe County and, at Lewisburg on August 28, routed a Federal force led by future president Colonel Rutherford B. Hayes.

Threatened by a much larger Union army, Wharton returned to Narrows. The 51st Regiment, now under the command of Lieutenant Colonel Augustus Forsberg, moved to Grey Sulphur Springs, where it drilled for several weeks and served on picket duty. In early September 1862, the brigade moved back into present day West Virginia and defeated a Federal force at Montgomery Ferry on the Kanawha River. It captured many supplies, including food, clothing, and arms.

The Confederates again occupied Charleston, driving the Federal forces toward the Ohio River. They camped for several weeks, enjoying the luxury of the captured supplies. Loring decided to move from Charleston back to the Greenbrier River. General Lee replaced him with General John Echols and ordered the unit back to Charleston, but a large Federal army already occupied the city. The brigade returned to Narrows, Virginia, where it remained for the winter of 1862-1863.

In March 1863, Colonel Wharton received orders from General Samuel Jones, commanding the Department of Western Virginia, to place his brigade where it could defend the lead mines, the salt wells, and the Virginia and Tennessee Railroad in southwest Virginia. He established headquarters at Glade Springs, Virginia. His command of 1,154 men included the 51st and 50th Virginia Regiments, the 30th Virginia Battalion of Infantry, and Stamp's Artillery.

Desertions became a severe problem, and recruitment of replacements became necessary. Lieutenant Woolwine headed a recruitment team that had some success getting sixteen men, found those making and selling whiskey, and returned six deserters from Company A in Russell and Wise counties.

In June 1863, the 51st moved into Tennessee to support General Buckner's forces near Chattanooga, where an expected attack did not appear. After two weeks, the regiment returned to Glade Springs. On June 27, Confederate cavalry drove away a Federal force at Saltville. Colonel Wharton reported that the 51st had 972 men.

After taking the train to Staunton, the troops marched to Woodstock and joined the Army of Northern Virginia under General Robert E. Lee on his march away from Gettysburg. On July 8, Wharton received a promotion to Brigadier General and Forsberg to Colonel of the 51st.

Early in August, General Lee ordered Wharton's Brigade to Warm Springs to block Federal General Averell's advance. Averell backed off and returned to West Virginia. During the summer of 1863, the 51st marched from Staunton to Glade Springs via Winchester, Orange Courthouse, Warm Springs, Dublin Depot, Abingdon, and Jonesboro, Tennessee.

Near the end of August, the brigade returned to southwest Virginia as the Federals made a determined effort to destroy the salt works, the lead mines, and the railroad. They captured Bristol and burned the town. The Confederates gathered all the forces they could get to oppose the Federals. At the last minute, the Union forces under General Burnside gave up the effort and returned to Knoxville. The Confederates pursued as far as Jonesboro, Tennessee.

General Robert Ransom assumed command of the Department of Western Virginia and Eastern Tennessee. He moved Wharton's Brigade to Blountville, Tennessee, to support General Longstreet, who was trying to recapture Knoxville. All during the autumn of 1863, the 51st marched and counter-marched in the Rogersville-Bean Station area of Tennessee between the Holston River and the Clinch Mountains, expecting contact with the enemy at all times but seeing little fighting.

In January 1864, the 51st marched in General Longstreet's failed attempt to trap a Federal force near Dandridge, Tennessee. Many of the men had no shoes, and their bleeding feet left red marks in the snow. The men spent much time foraging during the bitterly frigid winter, for in addition to food, they lacked good clothing and shelter. The harsh winter took the lives of many soldiers. In one month, the strength of Wharton's Brigade (including the 51st and 45th Regiments and 30th Battalion of

Infantry) dropped from 915 to 725 men.

The brigade, barely at the strength of a regiment, moved to Bull's Gap to protect the headquarters of the Department of East Tennessee in February. They repaired roads and performed picket duty. They had not seen battle in over a year.

Woolwine witnessed the execution of deserters in Tennessee. By February, he was back in Patrick County attending a "Frollick at Widow Celah Hubbard." He continued with a myriad of duties, from commanding the company in April to acting as adjutant to Lieutenant Colonel John Wolfe.

In April 1864, the regiment marched to Abingdon in terrible weather over the muddiest possible roads. Woolwine presided over the execution of a deserter, writing, "the regiment being formed in two battalions to march out to the execution of John H. Jones of 30th Battalion Sharp Shooters of Grayson County for desertion. He was executed at two o'clock p.m."

Early in May 1864, General Lee reorganized the Army of Southwest Virginia and placed General John C. Breckinridge, a former vice president of the United States, in charge. The 51st, stationed at Narrows, Virginia, transferred north to the Valley of Virginia on May 6, 1864, riding the train to Staunton and marching north, down the valley, to meet the oncoming Federals. Wharton pushed the brigade of 1557 men (including the 30th Virginia Infantry, the 62nd Mounted Infantry, and Company A of the 1st Missouri Cavalry along with the 51st) an amazing 187 miles in 8 days.

On May 13, Wharton's Brigade, as part of Breckinridge's Division in the Army of Northern Virginia, halted two miles south of New Market. The cadets from Virginia Military Institute joined the brigade there. At the famous Battle of New Market, the 51st was on the front line in the thick of the fight under the command of Lieutenant Colonel John P. Wolfe, using the Keydets as reserves to drive the Federals from the field.

On May 15, Woolwine wrote, "at one o'clock company moved out for New Market in the county of Shenandoah. Day very inclement. Threw up rail works some two or three miles from

New Market. Enemy did not advance. Marched forward and attacked the town at 9 am. Whipped and drove the enemy across the North Fork of the Shenandoah River. They burnt the bridge. We captured many prisoners, five pieces of artillery, wagons, and small arms."

After New Market, General Lee ordered General Breckinridge's troops to proceed to Hanover County to aid in defense of Richmond. The entire regiment now numbered 588 men. They defended the Virginia Central Railroad junction with the Richmond, Fredericksburg, and Potomac lines. The 51st successfully prevented the bridge's destruction over the South Anna River and repelled a Federal attack near Henry Clay's birthplace on May 28. Companies A and D, led by Major William T. Akers, skirmished with Federal troops and lost four men.

After the Battle of the Wilderness, fighting continued throughout the area as General Grant engaged in his relentless campaign to wear down Lee's troops and capture Richmond. In the battles of Mechanicsville, Cold Harbor, and Frayser's Farm, the

51st suffered heavy losses.

Woolwine reported they took a train, the "General Stuart," and went to Hanover Junction. The 51st joined the Army of Northern Virginia. Woolwine wrote, "heavy skirmishing along the entire. Enemy moved last night. Great many troops coming in. Saw General R. E. Lee...Passed Ashland and camped near where Henry Clay was born." A few days later, he writes," Twenty ninth, Fortified. Thirtieth, some skirmishing...Thirty-first, Had to fall back under a galling fire. Joseph Rose killed. Heavy firing from artillery During the day sharpshooters kept very busy. June first, drove them from their rifle pits...That night we were relieved and marched to Mechanicsville. Slept a few hours and day dawned. Second, To Chickahominy. At Gaines Farm drove their sharpshooters from their pits and fortified. Third, at dawn of day enemy attacked General Echols. They were handsomely repulsed with great slaughter to them." This battle took its name from a local tavern named Cold Harbor.

On June 7, General Lee ordered Breckinridge's forces back

to the Shenandoah Valley to block the advance of the Federals under General David Hunter. Born in the Shenandoah Valley, Hunter, a militant abolitionist, seemed to relish punishing the Southerners. He burned much of Staunton and Buchanan, captured Lexington, and burned the Virginia Military Institute along with most of the town. His forces captured Liberty, now Bedford, and fully expected to capture Lynchburg, which served as the junction of the railroads on which their armies depended for arms and food; its capture would have been a serious blow to the Confederates.

General Wharton assumed temporary command of the division as Breckinridge recovered from wounds received at Cold Harbor, and the brigade took the train to Lynchburg. By June 16, the 51st built breastworks near Thomas Jefferson's Poplar Forest and, by various ruses such as marching and counter-marching for the next two days, outwitted General Hunter. After severe fighting, Hunter retreated from the city back toward Liberty. Confederate forces followed and engaged Hunter at Hanging Rock near Salem, defeating him.

In a month, the 51st assisted in repelling three superior armies at New Market, Cold Harbor, and Lynchburg. On June 16, Woolwine wrote, "Left an hour early and marched for Lynchburg, distant 13 miles. Passed through city to camp west of fair grounds. I went back to town and had quite a nice time."

The 51st, now a part of Franklin County native Jubal Early's command, serving in Wharton's Brigade, Echols' Division, chased Hunter into West Virginia. The regiment fought for Early in the Shenandoah Valley Campaign of 1864. They marched almost constantly for three months, and Woolwine rose in rank from first lieutenant to captain.

Late in June 1864, the army started down the Shenandoah Valley and reached Winchester in early July. It captured enormous quantities of food and other supplies abandoned by the retreating Federal forces. After a day's rest, plenty of food, and some new clothes, the 51st marched to Martinsburg, where it chased away a Federal force under General Franz Sigel. After crossing the

Potomac River and routing several more Federal forces, it proceeded toward Washington. On July 8, the regiment repelled an attack at Middletown as fighting occurred at the Battle of Monocacy.

Woolwine reports on July 9, 1864, "On to Frederick City. Layed in line of battle all day. Gordon's division whipped the enemy. We crossed Monocosy (Monocacy) River, camped for the night." On the Eleventh, he wrote, "Went within 5 miles of city Washington." Echols Division guarded the trains, and although ordered up it never engaged in the fighting. A few days later, Rufus wrote, "Heard sermon from third chapter 18th verse James by Rev Brillheart on the bank of the Opequon." The verse ironically reads, "And the fruit of righteousness is sown in peace of them that make peace."

On July 10, the army camped only five miles from Washington. The regiment remained there two days within sight of the Federal Capital. General Early thought it too risky due to the large Federal forces on their way to protect the city. He crossed the Potomac into Virginia, where he encountered and defeated several small Federal forces. Temporarily, all Federal forces were out of the Shenandoah Valley. Shortly after that, General Early's cavalry crossed back over the Potomac and burned the town of Chambersburg, Pennsylvania, in retaliation for General Hunter's burning of Staunton, Lexington, and Buchanan. The 51st stayed near Sharpsburg, Maryland, while McCausland burned Chambersburg. Early's men returned to Virginia and camped in the Winchester area.

In August 1864, General Philip Sheridan assumed command of the Federal forces and launched an offensive against Early in the Shenandoah Valley. He began a relentless campaign that destroyed the Valley. General Early's troops retreated south up the Valley in a series of battles.

Woolwine wrote on August 12, "Left before day. Moved on in direction of Strasburg, passing Middletown. Formed line of Battle on Hupp's Hill near Strasburg. Some skirmishing. Remained all day. At night to Fisher's Hill. Formed our command on right of road. Thirteenth through the seventeenth threw up some works. Some skirmishing. Seventieth, the enemy had gone. Pursued and fought at Winchester. Took the fort. Lost of 51st was 3 killed, 28 wounded. Ladies met us on the field."

On August 22, while Early advanced up to the Maryland line, Woolwine wrote, "stopped our brigade at an old church known as Trinity church, built during the reign of Ann Queen of England. In rear of the crumbling structure and dilapidated walls is a grave with the following inscription: 'Sacred to the memory of John Baker who departed this life May 30, 1798, aged 67 years.' I went to town and saw the identical spot where justice overtook John Brown." He witnessed the twenty-second execution of a fellow Confederate for desertion.

On August 25, he wrote, "Moved out at sunrise, crossed fields and old road. Struck pike at Leetown. We passed beyond church. Loaded. Sent 51st forward as skirmishers. Engaged the enemy and drove them a piece. Enemy flanked us and we had to fall back. Our loss in killed, wounded and captured was 102. Lt Col

Wolfe and Lt John Akers were among the slain." The next day he wrote, "We moved back by the old battleground, passed the usual horrors of war, over Col. (John P.) Wolfe's grave and went to church and camped for the night."

Picket duty occupied the 51st from September 15 until the nineteenth at Stephenson's Depot near Winchester. Heavy fighting occurred with heavy losses. Members of the 51st scattered several times, and a number fell into enemy hands. During the fighting around Winchester, William Tyler Akers received a promotion to major and commanded the 51st Regiment for a time. R. J. Woolwine replaced him as captain of Company D. The Confederates won some skirmishes but could not hold out against Sheridan's relentless pressure from far superior numbers.

During September, Woolwine and the 51st fought at Fisher's Hill on September 22 with Wharton's Brigade (including the 45th Virginia and the 30th Battalion of Infantry). The regiment was the size of a company, and the brigade had only 417 men.

Woolwine wrote on the nineteenth, "enemy attacked flanks of Thirtieth Virginia Battalion. We fell back and formed our line nearer town and repulsed them several times ordered to Winchester, then move to rear and repulsed enemy. Our line was giving way, but we fell back in good order to our works. From there we got out in great confusion. Loss heavy. Continued the retreat...sent to Strasburg to stop stragglers. During engagement enemy rode over me and I captured a horse and came out on it. The same was stolen from me at Strasburg. Loss was five kelled fifty five wounded and seventy four captured." On the twenty-second he wrote of the Battle of Fisher's Hill, "I received the order announcing my promotion to the Captaincy of Co D. We stampeded." Three of the 51st died, and 28 were wounded.

Reinforcements joined the brigade while it waited for a chance to go on the offensive. On October 13, 1864, the Confederates reentered the Valley and marched toward Winchester, where they encountered Sheridan's army at Cedar Creek.

At first, General Early's troops drove back the Federals. The 51st, led by Major W. T. Akers, charged a Federal entrenchment and succeeded in driving the Federals away, but superior strength prevailed, and Major Akers' forces fell back. The Union Sixth Corps and cavalry wrecked the 51st. The retreat soon turned into confusion that resulted in a rout. General Early retreated up the Valley to New Market. Woolwine wrote of the Battle of Cedar Creek on October 19, "Moved out at one o'clock a. m. Some of the army flanked. We moved in front and drove enemy out of their camp on the hill at Cedar Creek. But at 4:30 p.m. the tide of battle turned, and we fled the field back to Fisher's Hill."

Later that month, Woolwine wrote, "Took train for Richmond, Visited soldier's home and Camp Lee." During November and December, he reported, "Snowed and Hailed...On working detail. Had the misfortune to get one man killed. Private Henry Lindsey Co. I, 50th Regiment, Carroll County Va. 45th Virginia Regiment refused to drill 51st went to arrest those that refused to drill, my Company took possession of their arms...I took command of the 45 Regiment."

The 51st moved to New Market and into winter quarters. On December 16, Wharton's men, the only Confederates left in the Shenandoah Valley, moved to Fishersville in Augusta County. Since June 1864, the 51st had marched 1,670 miles and participated in 75 battles or skirmishes.

In January, Fishersville Woolwine wrote, "Where oh where shall I be twelve months hence? Perhaps in vast eternity. All are now taking their sweet repose. Lt. Cheely and myself are enjoying ourselves eating fine apples. Have just completed my pay rolls." He returned to Patrick County for almost a month in January and February 1865, continuing to attend "Frollicks." His uncle, Notley P. Adams, sent General Early $250 in Confederate money.

The Battle of Waynesboro on March 2, 1865, began with sleet and snow falling as the regiment prepared to cross the North Fork of the Shenandoah River. Wharton reported that his division (including the 45th, 50th, and 51st Virginia Regiments and 30th

Battalion Virginia Infantry) had 800 men against 7500 "splendidly equipped" Federal cavalry under the immediate command of George Custer and overall command of Phillip Sheridan. Colonel Forsberg commanded the brigade with Major Akers commanding the 51st on its last battlefield. The cavalry surrounded them, and most of the regiment surrendered. Woolwine wrote, "There we was all captured."

While the following list may not be complete, the men listed from Patrick County were captured at Waynesboro and spent the remainder of the war in Federal prisons: George M. Agee, William Tyler Akers, Carr Allen, John V. Anthony, John W. Bowling, Thomas J. Burroughs, Stephen M. Cannaday, John R. Clark, John Conner, John M. Cruise, Samuel W. Davis, Pleasant DeHart, Thomas J. DeHart, Thomas T. DeHart, Peyton Foley, James Franklin Hall, Thomas R. Hall, John T. Hancock, Peter Handy, William T. Harris, Eden T. Hatcher, Elkanah Hatcher, Harvey D. Hopkins, James M. Hopkins, Caleb Howell, Jonathan W. Hubbard, Thomas M. Hubbard, William J. Jefferson, Naamon W. Knowles,

James M. Lawson, David H. Martin, Edward N. Martin, T. J. Martin, Green McGee, James Tyler Morrison, John Tatum Morrison, Robert Moss, Charles M. Nolen, Valentine Hamson Pendleton, Paul C. Pigg, Thomas C. Pigg, Richard R. Rakes, George W. Reynolds, William A. Reynolds, Landon Roberson, John W. Rorrer, William T. Ross, John Salmons, John W. Scott, Samuel Scott, Lewis T. Thomas, James R. Turner, Tazewell A. Turner, Elijah DeHart Via, J. Williams and Rufus James Woolwine.

Rufus Woolwine's career as a soldier for the Confederate States of America was over. He served from the very beginning in 1861 and fought to within one month of the end. He saw twenty-two men executed for desertion. His duties included recruiting, chasing deserters, catching whiskey makers, acting as a messenger, and fighting beside his men as an infantryman.

General Wharton and the rest of the 51st Virginia joined the Army of Northern Virginia and served under General John B. Gordon. Forces of the United States captured most of those left along with their battle flag on March 25 at Fort Stedman.

Wharton went to Lynchburg to defend the city and was at Christiansburg on April 10 when he heard of Lee's surrender. The 51st Virginia Infantry Regiment disbanded that day.

After the war, Wharton lived and married in Radford, Virginia. He served two terms in the Virginia Senate, where he was involved in creating Virginia Tech. When he died in 1906, his family wrapped him in the battle flag of the 51st Virginia Infantry Regiment.

**A replica of the battle flag of the 51st Virginia Infantry buried with Gabriel Wharton.**

The prisoners from Waynesboro marched to Staunton, Winchester, and Harper's Ferry and then to prisons at Elmira, New York, and Fort Delaware. Captain Woolwine and most of his company went to Fort Delaware. On March 9, he wrote of leaving Harper's Ferry, traveling to Baltimore, and staying in prison at Fort McHenry, the site of Francis Scott Key's immortal poem that is today our national anthem.

Fort Delaware, completed in 1859 after ten years of construction, is today a state park on Pea Patch Island in the Delaware River outside present day Wilmington. The river is ten miles wide at the site halfway between New Jersey and Delaware. Brigadier General Alban F. Schoepf commanded the prison when the members of the 51st Virginia Infantry arrived on March 11, 1865. Schoepf, born in Poland in 1822 and educated in Vienna, served in the Austrian army until he joined a failed Hungarian revolt. He escaped to Syria and made his way to North America in 1851. After working in the U. S. Patent Office and War Department, he fought early in the war in Kentucky.

Prison life at Fort Delaware involved living in a T-shaped barracks divided for officers and enlisted men. Described as lice-infested in the summer and bitterly cold in the winter, the quarters consisted of bunks stacked four high. Food for a day consisted of "one small loaf of bread and one small piece of meat, together with a half pint or sometimes a pint of weak vegetable juice soup." The following is a stanza of a song rendered by the prisoners at Fort Delaware.

"Now white folks here's a moral; dars nothing true below

For life is but a tater patch, the debil has to hoe

Ebery one has his troubles here, tho's he go near and far,

But the most unlucky debil, is the prisoner of war."

During Woolwine's imprisonment, he continued writing: "March 24th, drawn one pair of drawers. 25th, drawn one pair socks. April third, Drawn one blanket, 1 pair drawers, heard of the fall of Richmond. Fourth salute fired." On the twentieth, he wrote, "Where will Lt (John M.) Cemise and myself be one month hence? At home well and hearty I fondly hope." On the twenty-sixth, he wrote, "Oh what a lovely day. How much I wish I was in old Patrick this beautiful evening. At _____ with Miss _____, yes the beautiful accomplished _____. The sole subject of all my earthly affection. Oh what a proud consolation it would be to know that she is well and still thinks of her absent, as well as unchanging friend, Rufus." He read books in prison, including The New Testament, The Wild West Scenes, Tempest and Sunshine, and volume one of The Conquest of Mexico.

Religion continued to be a strong theme in his writing. On Sunday, the 30th, he wrote, "Glad would I be to quit the life of a prisoner of war and return to my quiet home in the mountains of Patrick. There to rest from the cares and troubles of a four years hard campaigning. I'll trust a merciful god. Myself and Captain Dobyns expects to be at home to day one month hence." On Sunday, May 14, Woolwine wrote of the Charity meeting, "Oh how much I wish I was there. To mingle with old friends that I love so much. I truly hope to be there at the next meeting." The next day he wrote, "My motto is Trust to Luck. Would like to exchange my present abode for my home in old Patrick. Just had a pleasant nap. I was far far away from here in my dreams." The following Sunday, he wrote, "Today is Jack Creek meeting. Wish I was there to mingle with friends and relatives, but alas! I see no prospects of a speedy release from this place. Well! I await patiently the action of the government...From this time forward I shall earnestly endeavor to quit the habit of using tobacco in any way whatever." Sprinkled among his writings were quotes in Latin such as "Whilst I Breathe I Hope" and "Never Despair."

Dr. James A. Davis, President of Shenandoah University, wrote in the *51st Virginia Infantry Regiment* that these men came home to "no cheering crowds or clanging bands" but to "broken fences and fields of weeds." They fought the "forgotten war." Seldom were they with Lee and the Army of Northern Virginia, but they were protecting southwestern Virginia's salt works and railroads. They experienced everything imaginable, including death, disease, desertion, harsh weather, and fighting without supplies and the full strength of manpower. In battle, they cleared an escape route from Fort Donelson, saw victory at New Market, and marched within five miles of Washington D. C. with Jubal Early. These men did not fail in their cause because they lacked courage or skill as fighters. Those who survived moved on with the remainder of their lives.

Woolwine took the Oath of Allegiance on June 17, 1865, and began his return to Patrick County two days later on the steamer "Richard Willing." He arrived home on June 27 after a trip that took him from Baltimore via water to Newport News and Richmond, where he saw Washington's statue on the Capitol grounds "draped in mourning." As he traveled by railroad toward Lynchburg, he had to get off at Burke's Station and walk, then catch another train to Farmville. He rode the last five miles to Lynchburg on the James River and Kanawha Canal, then caught a train to Elliston and walked home from there. Woolwine ended his journal with these thoughts: "Thus ends a journey of four years through the most eventful campaign known in the history of men or nations. Now that peace once more smiles upon our land and country, let us look to the wise disposer of all human events and implore Him in His infinite wisdom and mercy to smile upon and bless us, a subjugated people. God grant that our course may be such as to meet with the hearty approval of those in authority, both on earth and in heaven. Oh! That we may yield placid obedience to the laws of our land and the laws of God, so that we may again place our dear old state in her original high standing. And when we shall have done this and have finished our pilgrimage here below, may we all join that celestial host of angels in bright glory to sing praises forever more, to the great Jehovah."

Woolwine settled on Russell Creek in Patrick County, where he manufactured tobacco and sold dry goods. In 1866, he became deputy sheriff of Patrick County. He married Sarah R. Brown in 1868. She received attention from R. J. Reynolds but chose Woolwine because he had visited her in college. They had four children: Sallie, who married M. V. Stedman; Ada, who married H. S. McKinley; Mabel, who married J. C. Barksdale; and Rufus E. Woolwine, who served as commonwealth attorney of Patrick County for twenty years.

Former Captain Woolwine moved to Stuart and served as sheriff from 1891 until 1904. He lived in retirement until his death on December 4, 1908. The old soldier rests in the Stuart Cemetery near his messmate William Dennis Via. For thirty years, Woolwine

served as secretary of the Sunday school at Stuart Methodist

Church, where his favorite hymn was "A Charge To Keep I Have."

Rufus James Woolwine lived as a good citizen, obeying and

enforcing the laws. He put the war behind him but left his

thoughts and feelings to give us insight into a momentous time in

our history.

On December 6, 1900, an aging man from Sweden rose to

speak to the Garland Rodes Camp of the United Confederate

Veterans in Lynchburg. Augustus Forsberg said, "Many years have

passed since the events I have just narrated, and, like similar

details of warfare, not of such importance as to merit a place in

history, they will soon be forgotten. But the participants in the

struggle of those 'days that tried men's souls' cannot readily

forget the trials and perils to which they were exposed."

In July 1913, President Woodrow Wilson presided over the

fiftieth anniversary of the Battle of Gettysburg. As a young boy,

Wilson, a native Virginian, saw Jefferson Davis brought through

Augusta, Georgia, after the Confederate President's capture. This memory was still strong when Wilson spoke at this historic moment saying, "We are made by these tragic, epic things to know what it costs to make a nation—the blood and sacrifice of multitudes of unknown men lifted to a great stature in the view of all generations by knowing no limit to their manly willingness to serve." One North and South veteran represented each side on the platform near Wilson. In a symbolic gesture of reunification, the President simultaneously grasped both men's hands. Photographs show Dr. William Dennis Via of Patrick County, the Southern soldier holding a Second National Flag of the Confederacy on display in the Patrick County Historical Museum.

Born on September 8, 1838, Via enlisted in the Ross Company of the 51st Virginia Infantry in June 1861, serving with Rufus Woolwine. After the war, he married Minnie Via and had five children: Daisy, James, Marcie, Mary, and Posie. Dr. Via, a dentist, served as one of the first Trustees of the town of Stuart and possibly mayor in 1884. Less than a year before his death, the old soldier still attended reunions, the last one in Jacksonville,

Florida. As the last survivor of his mess, his time as Corporal, Company D, 51st Virginia Infantry dominated his thoughts. Dr. Via died on March 6, 1915, and lies today in Stuart town Cemetery near his friend, Rufus James Woolwine. On February 20, 1914, reflecting upon the death of his friend Via authored the following poem and sent it to Woolwine's daughter.

"Oh! Death thou has taken him away,

 And his suffering was so great.

I stayed with him all I could,

 For he was my last 'messmate'!

My 'mess' have all left me now,

 And I am left here alone.

Captain Woolwine, the last to leave me,

 Our friendship was truly known!

We traveled over mountains and valleys,

 Where crystal streams ran down.

Now all their travelings are over,

 Not one of them can be found!

The Lord has done right with them

    I hope they are all at rest.

Though I am left here alone,

    I hope they are with the blest!

If they are with their Saviour,

    Though I cannot long here remain.

My 'mess' has gone and left me,

    Though true happiness I hope to gain!

We loved and respected each other,

    While we together roamed.

But they have all left me now,

    And I will seek a heavenly home!

Now I hope to meet them all,

    In the sweet bye and bye.

And walk the golden streets of heaven,

    Where we will never, never die

The 1903 Confederate Reunion in Patrick County. Rufus Woolwine is wearing the bowler hat on the far left, second from the end. President Thomas Woodrow Wilson and William Dennis Via of Patrick County and the 51st Virginia Infantry at the Gettysburg Reunion in 1913.

# PART THREE

# THE GOVERNOR

"This is the most remarkable case that has been presented to me for consideration...He (Notley P. Adams) has been a most litigious man, generally successful in his controversies and has therefore rendered himself if not absolutely odious, at least highly improper."

Virginia Governor John Letcher, 1863

# Chapter Six

## Enter The Governor

John Letcher, the Civil War Governor of Virginia, was born on March 29, 1813, in Lexington, Virginia. A cousin of Patrick County native James Ewell Brown "Jeb" Stuart, the Confederate Major General, who served as commander of Robert E. Lee's cavalry in the Army of Northern Virginia. Stuart's great-grandfather was William Letcher, who is buried in the oldest marked grave in Patrick County. During the American Revolution, William lost his life in August 1780 to Tories, pro-British sympathizers.

John Letcher went to Randolph Macon College and graduated from Washington Academy in 1833. He studied law and attended Virginia Constitutional Convention in 1850 with his kinsman Archibald Stuart, father of J. E. B. Stuart. Letcher served in the United States House of Representatives from 1853-59. Elected Governor in 1859, right after John Brown raided Harper's Ferry and oversaw Virginia secession when he refused to send troops to Washington when Abraham Lincoln requested them to put down the "rebellion" after the firing on Fort Sumter.

Letcher unsuccessfully ran for the Confederate Congress. In 1865, United States authorities imprisoned him for two months. He served two years in the Virginia Legislature and over a decade on the Board of Visitors at the Virginia Military Institute. Letcher died on January 26, 1884.

On October 6, 1863, Judge Fulton wrote to Governor John Letcher stating that the stress of bail, bad health, and the slight suspicion of guilt led him to believe that Adams deserved consideration of a pardon.

On October 8, 1863, William Burwell wrote to Governor Letcher stating that "Adams told me that on his way home the evening the house was burnt that he saw several persons engaged about this domestic concerns and what particular acts they were engaged in for instance he saw one farmer some distance from the road burning log heaps and that there were two women with him that he hollered to him. I sent for this man, and he confirmed the fact. Another was passing from his house to the stable with a turn of fodder on his head and Adams hear his wife ask him why he was so late getting home. Another house some 2 to 300 yards from road, Adams saw two persons passing from the kitchen to the dwelling house with alight to the house."

On November 6, 1863, William Burwell wrote to Virginia Governor John Letcher for Adams's release stating that the Sheriff, Deputies, Commonwealth Attorney, and County Clerk were all "avowed and notorious" enemies and implied they conspired against Adams. Burwell stated the charge ought not to be sustained against Adams.

Adams stated that he saw several persons engaged in domestic concerns. Someone was burning logs with two women and another going from the house to the stable with fodder. Two people at another house were going from the house to the kitchen.

Four days later, on November 10, 1863, W. A. Patterson, the Surgeon of the Virginia Penitentiary, wrote of Adams that he was of the "greatest mental disquietude, suffering mental agony and weeps at once if kindly spoken too. He is not at all a lunatic in my opinion, but a great sufferer from incarceration."

William Burwell indicated that Adams was suffering from depression, causing "near insanity," in a letter dated November 6, 1863. Burwell continued, "I ask in his name and in the name of justice that he be relieved as early as possible...Sheriff and deputies, clerks, Commonwealth Attorneys and others in office are his enemies and exert an influence over his destiny and trial...He is a persecuted man, and that his prayers when he cries 'deliver me from my enemies or I will perish.'"

Four Days Later, John E. Penn wrote Burwell, stating, "the charge against Notley P. Adams ought not to have been sustained...the prosecution and most of their witnesses were avowed and notorious enemies of Adams." Penn was a Colonel in command of the 42nd Virginia Infantry who lost a leg at Sharpsburg, Maryland, along the banks of Antietam Creek.

This set off a firestorm of petitions in Patrick County. Those against Adam's release were Sheriff Turner. It was suggested that the Justice of the Peace for bail was an uncle of the sheriff and had a conflict of interest.

Eighty people in Henry County petitioned for pardon, believing that a "group" decided it was Notley P. Adams that committed the crime before the evidence was examined. Fifty people from Danville, Virginia, petitioned Governor Letcher for Adam's release. Other petitions stated that Adams could not get a fair trial.

Governor Letcher received a petition with four hundred signatures asking him not to pardon Adams. This group included Sheriff Turner, Jacob Clark, John Martin, Ed Fulcher, John Wood, John Yates, John DeHart, Jeffrey Giles, Matthew Arnold, Harry Hopkins, J. D. Mitchell, James Shockley, and others.

Patrick County petitions continued to arrive, with one representing twenty-eight people who believed Adams could not get a fair trial and twenty believing he could receive a fair trial.

L. J. Wray wrote Governor Letcher on December 16, 1863, that there was evidence for a conviction.

## December 23<sup>rd</sup>, 1863, Richmond, Virginia

In the year 1859 Notley P. Adams charged with intentionally setting fire to a dwelling house was arrested and regularly indicted in the Circuit Court of Patrick County. This is the most remarkable case that has been presented to me for consideration. The party was twice admitted to bail by Judge Fulton after a full and patient hearing of the testimony was entirely insufficient to warrant a conviction. The case was once tried, and the jury failed to agree. This trial was held before Judge Gilmer. It was again tried before the late Judge Fulkerson, when the jury found the prisoner guilty, and ascertained the term of his imprisonment at three years in the penitentiary The Judge set aside the verdict on the grounds that it was not justified by the evidence. He repeatedly declared. I learn from Honorable W. R. Staples, that he did not return the prisoner was guilty, and that he felt it to be his duty as a Judge to set aside any verdict of correction. The final trial was held before Judge ___ last fall and the prisoner was found guilty and sentenced to three years imprisonment, and as now undergoing punishment.

The evidence in the case is as circumstantial, and I am satisfied from the conflicting testimony, that there is great room for doubt as to his guilt. It cannot fail I think to be clearly manifest to anyone who will examine the papers on file in the support of the application for pardon, that passion and prejudice have controlled the public sentiment of the country, and the ends of justice I think demanded that the venue should have been changed.

He has been a most litigious man, generally successful in his controversies and has therefore rendered himself if not absolutely odious at best highly unpopular. He as a large interesting and as I understand respectable family. He is upwards of sixty years of age, and quite infirm.

Under a full review therefore of all the circumstances, I direct his discharge.

John Letcher, Governor of Virginia

December 23rd 1863

In the year 1859 Notty P Adams charged with unlawfully setting fire to a dwelling house was arrested, and regularly indicted in the Circuit Court of Patrick County. This is the most remarkable case, that has been presented to me for consideration. This party was twice admitted to bail by Judge Fulton after a full and patient hearing of the testimony, and I understand has repeatedly declared that the testimony was entirely insufficient to warrant a conviction. The case was once tried, and the jury failed to agree. This trial was had before Judge Gilmer. It was again tried before the late Judge Fulkerson, when the jury found the prisoner and ascertained the term of his imprisonment at three years in the penitentiary. The Judge set aside the verdict on the ground that it was not justified by the evidence. He repeatedly declared I learn from Hon W R Staples, that he did not believe the prisoner was guilty, and that he felt it to be his duty as a Judge to set aside any verdict of conviction. The final trial was had before Judge Wingfield last fall and the prisoner was found guilty and sentenced to three years imprisonment, and is now undergoing punishment.

The evidence in the case is cir

122

circumstantial, and I am satisfied from the conflicting testimony, that there is great room for doubt as to his guilt. It cannot fail I think to be clearly manifest to any one who will examine the papers on file in support of the application for pardon, that passion and prejudice have controlled the public sentiment of the country, and the ends of justice I think demanded that the venue should have been changed.

He has been a most litigious man, generally successful in his controversies, and has therefore rendered himself, if not absolutely odious, at least highly unpopular. He has a large, interesting and as I understand respectable family. He is upwards of sixty years of age, and quite infirm.

Under a full view therefore of all the circumstances, I direct his discharge

John Letcher

Notley P. Adams continued his litigious nature after the War Between The States. On three consecutive Februarys in 1865, 1866, and 1867, he escaped from the Patrick County jail. The Order Books in the courthouse are full of Adams' post war career.

Order Book #10 tells of cases versus Green and Samuel Harris in 1869 and again in 1871. Order Book #11 has nine different mentions of Adams, such as fines of $5 for contempt. There were charges for stealing Green Connor's horse and $100 worth of goods. He challenged James E. Via to a duel after a grand jury indictment of assault and battery. He sued Rufus Turner's estate, and in January 1869, Adams sued against "road changes."

In 1870, the Census has Celia living with Isaac Houchens. Notley was listed as age 68 and worth $5,000, living in the Smith River District.

Notley Price Adams died on November 15, 1882, in the custody of the Sheriff of Patrick County of what was described as a "deranged mind."

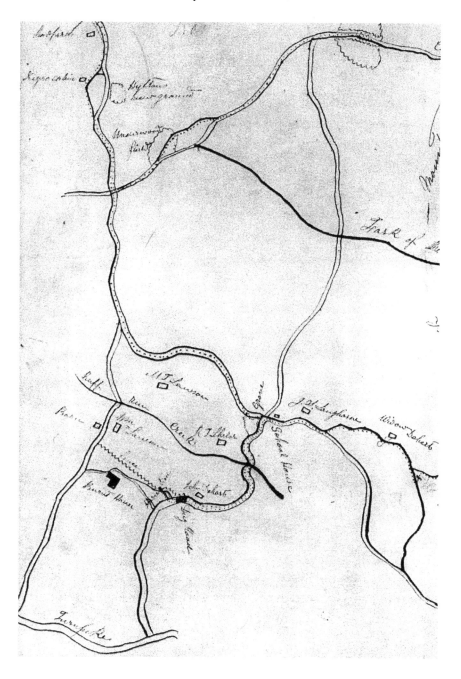

125

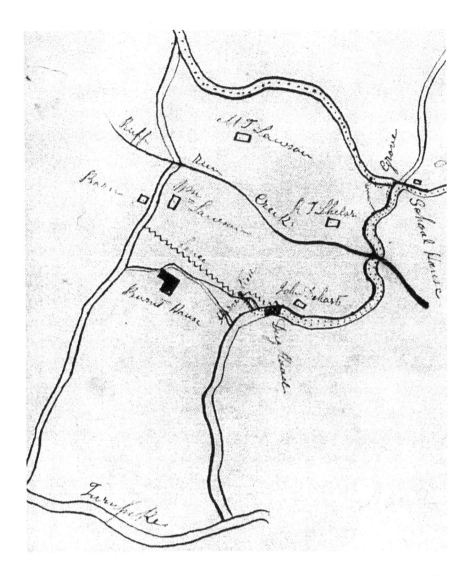

The "Burnt House" that Notley Price Adams was accused of burning was located in the roads Split Rail, Helms and Dehart just north of Meadows of Dan, Patrick County, Virginia.

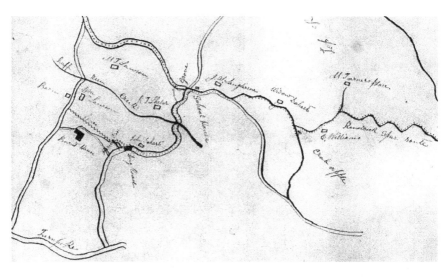

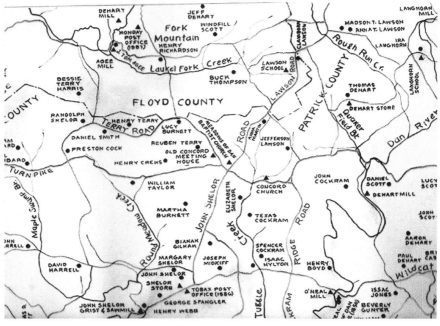

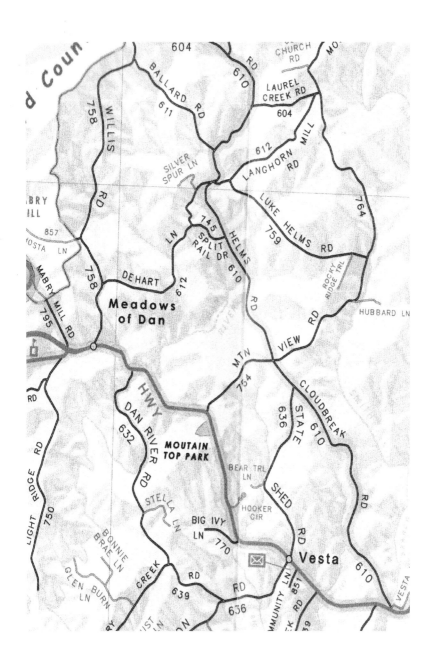

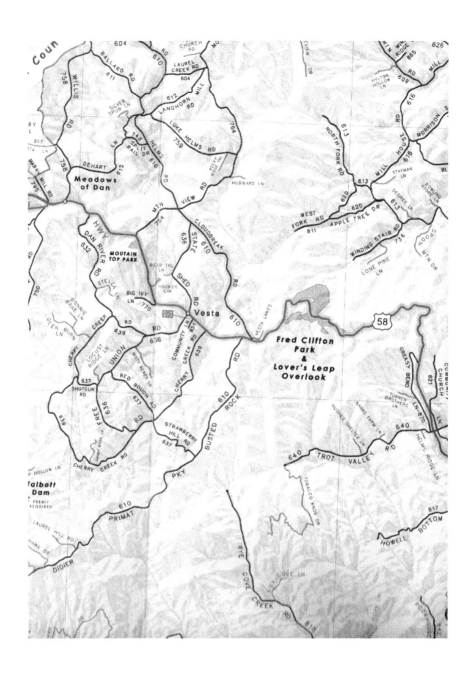

132

The papers relating to The Strange Case of Not Adams are
located in the Library of Virginia on Broad Street in Richmond.

## Selected Bibliography

Manuscripts

Library of Virginia
  Executive Papers of Governor John Letcher
  Series I: Chronological Files, 1859-1863
  Folder 1-3
  Miscellaneous Reel 4784, Box 29, December 1863.

  Chancery Causes
    Notley P. Adams vs. Walter R. Staples, 1871
    Notley P. Adams vs. Polly West

Virginia Tech
  Thomas David Perry Collection

Patrick County Virginia Courthouse
  Order Books # 8, 10, 12

Bassett Historical Center
  O. E. Pilson Papers

Census of the United States
  1850, 1860, 1870

Books and Articles

The Strange Case of Not Adams, Virginia Cavalcade

Manarin, Louis H. "The Civil War Diary of Rufus J. Woolwine." The Virginia Magazine of History and Biography, Volume 71, (4) October 1963:416-448.

Historian Thomas D. "Tom" Perry at the site he saved, J. E. B. Stuart's
Birthplace, the Laurel Hill Farm, just outside Mount Airy in Ararat,
Patrick County, Virginia.

# About The Author

J. E. B. Stuart's biographer, Emory Thomas, describes Tom Perry as "a fine and generous gentleman who grew up near Laurel Hill, where Stuart grew up, has founded J. E. B. Stuart Birthplace, and attracted considerable interest in the preservation of Laurel Hill. He has started a symposium series about aspects of Stuart's life to sustain interest in Stuart beyond Ararat, Virginia." Perry graduated from Patrick County High School in 1979 and Virginia Tech in 1983 with a bachelor's degree in history.

Tom founded the J. E. B. Stuart Birthplace in 1990. The non-profit organization has preserved 75 acres of the Stuart property, including the house site where J. E. B. Stuart was born on February 6, 1833. Perry wrote the original eight interpretive signs about Laurel Hill's history along with the Virginia Civil War Trails sign and the new Virginia Historical Highway Marker in 2002. He spent many years researching and traveling all over the nation to find Stuart materials. He continues his work to preserve Stuart's Birthplace, producing the Laurel Hill Teacher's Guide for educators and the Laurel Hill Reference Guide for groups.

Perry can be seen on Virginia Public Television's Forgotten Battlefields: The Civil War in Southwest Virginia with his mentor, noted Civil War Historian Dr. James I. Robertson, Jr. Perry has begun a collection of papers relating to Stuart and Patrick County history in the Special Collections Department of the Carol M. Newman Library at Virginia Tech under the auspices of the Virginia Center for Civil War Studies.

Historian Thomas D. Perry is the author and publisher of over forty books on regional history in Virginia surrounding his home county of Patrick. He is the author of ten books on Patrick County, Virginia, including Ascent to Glory, The Genealogy of J. E. B. Stuart, The Free State of Patrick: Patrick County Virginia in the Civil War, The Dear Old Hills of Patrick: J. E. B. Stuart and Patrick County, Virginia, Images of America: Patrick County Virginia, and Notes From The Free State Of Patrick.

For a decade, Perry taught Civil War history to every eleventh-grade history class at his alma mater, Patrick County High School, from his book The Free State of Patrick: Patrick County Virginia in the Civil War. He can be seen on Henrico County Virginia's DVD documentary Bold Dragoon: The Life of J. E. B. Stuart.

http://henrico-va.granicus.com/MediaPlayer.php?clip_id=1088

Perry was a featured presenter at the Virginia Festival of the Book in 2012. He speaks all over the country on topics ranging from Andy Griffith to J. E. B. Stuart.

In 2004, Perry began The Free State of Patrick Internet History Group, which became the largest historical organization in the area, with over 500 members. It covered Patrick County, Virginia, and regional history. Tom produced a monthly email newsletter about regional history entitled Notes From The Free State of Patrick.

In 2009, Perry used his book Images of America Henry County Virginia to raise over $25,000 for the Bassett Historical Center, "The Best Little Library in Virginia," and as editor of the Henry County Heritage Book, he raised another $30,000. Perry was responsible for over $200,000 of the $800,000 raised to expand the regional history library.

He is the recipient of the John E. Divine Award from the Civil War Education Association, the Hester Jackson Award from the Surry County Civil War Round Table, and the Best Article Award from the Society of North Carolina Historians for his article on Stoneman's Raid in 2008. In 2010, he received acknowledgment from the Bassett Public Library Association for his work to expand the Bassett Historical Center and was named Henry County Virginia Man of the Year by www.myhenrycounty.com. The Sons of the American Revolution presented Tom with the Good Citizenship Award. Perry also recently received the National Society of the Daughters of the American Revolution Community Service Award from the Patrick Henry Daughters of the American Revolution.

Perry has remembered the history of those who helped him. He worked with the Virginia Department of Transportation to name the bridge over the Dan River after his neighbor, Command Sergeant Major Zeb Stuart Scales, the most decorated non-commissioned soldier from Patrick County, Virginia. Perry remembered his teachers at Blue Ridge Elementary School, including his father, Erie Perry, who was a teacher and principal for thirty years in The Free State of Patrick, by placing a monument to the retired teachers at the school in Ararat, Virginia.

Perry, a recognized authority on J. E. B. Stuart, is working on a three-volume project titled The Papers of J. E. B. Stuart.

Made in the USA
Middletown, DE
20 July 2022

69531116R00080